For Eternity

Robert Cardinal Sarah

For Eternity

Restoring the Priesthood and Our Spiritual Fatherhood

Translated by Michael J. Miller

EWTN Publishing, Inc.
Irondale, Alabama

EWTN Publishing, Inc.
5817 Old Leeds Road, Irondale, AL 35210

Distributed by Sophia Institute Press, Box 5284, Manchester, NH 03108.

paperback ISBN 978-1-68278-291-0

ebook ISBN 978-1-68278-292-7

Library of Congress Control Number: 2022933505

First printing

To all seminarians throughout the world

Contents

Introduction

"I Come Humbly"

I come humbly to each one of you, as a brother, a friend, a father, and a fellow disciple of Jesus Christ. I come to meditate with you on this marvelous gift that has been given to us: the priesthood. Jesus Christ makes us participate in His priesthood in an extraordinary and undeserved way.

In the Church, the days of priestly ordinations are festive days. What a joy to see these young priests happy to give themselves to the Lord! Is there anyone who has not noticed and admired the profound joy on the wrinkled, weary faces of the old priests who have been faithful for so many years? The priestly ministry is a source of joy because it consists of giving divine life and leading souls to Heaven, to perfect joy.

Even so, in our times, the dark of night hangs over the lives of priests. Not a week goes by without a case of sexual abuse or corruption coming to light. We have to look at the truth head-on: the priesthood seems to be failing. Some priests are like sailors whose ship is being tossed violently by the storm. They whirl around and stagger. How can you help wondering about it when you read some accounts of child abuse? How can you not doubt? The priesthood, its status, its mission, and its authority have been placed at the service of the worst crimes. The priesthood has been exploited to hide, conceal, and even to justify the profanation of children's innocence. Episcopal authority has sometimes been utilized to pervert and even ruin the generosity of those who wanted to consecrate themselves to God. The search for worldly glory, power, honors, earthly pleasures, and money has infiltrated the hearts of priests, bishops, and cardinals. How can we tolerate such deeds without trembling, without weeping, without asking ourselves probing questions?

We cannot act as if all this was nothing to be concerned about; as if all this was just a routine hiccup. We have to look this evil in the face. Why is there so much corruption, straying, and perversion?

It is legitimate for others to demand an accounting of us. It is legitimate for the world to say to us: "You are like the Pharisees: you preach but you do not practice" (cf. Mt 23:3). The people of God look at their priests with suspicion. Unbelievers despise them and distrust them.

Some ask themselves whether the priesthood itself is not in doubt. Here and there we see proposals crop up to change the institution, to renew it, to modernize it. All these initiatives would be legitimate if the priesthood were a human institution. But we did not invent the priesthood; it is a gift from God. You do not reform a divine gift by loading it down with human ideas so as to conform it to current tastes. On the contrary, you restore it by removing from it the layers of whitewash that prevent the original from revealing its splendor.

Unfortunately, some have used the priesthood to satisfy their desire to sin. They have hijacked the meaning of priestly ordination. They have perverted the very meaning of the words. For example, when we say that the priest is identified with Christ to the point of becoming "another Christ," we never give this statement a psychological sense. The priest is by no means all-powerful. No one owes him blind obedience. Being identified with Christ gives the priest no right at all to command others or to satisfy his whims. On the contrary, being another Christ obliges the priest to become the least of servants; being another Christ obliges the priest to have a chaste, unlimited respect for everyone; being another Christ obliges me to get up on the Cross. Ordination does not put us on a throne but on the Cross. Let us not allow a few perverts to steal from us the very beautiful and very demanding words of the Christian tradition. The mystical and spiritual identification of the priest with Christ leads to no abuse if it is lived out in truth. Let us not be afraid to restore to these very demanding words their profound meaning.

The priesthood obliges us to shine with holiness. "Indeed," Saint John Chrysostom declares, "the soul of the priest must be purer than the rays of the sun, so that the Holy Spirit might never abandon him, so that he may be able to say: I no longer live, but Christ lives in me."[1]

The priesthood is the Church's most valuable possession. It should irradiate the world with the light and holiness of God. No sanctification is possible without the priesthood, "for just as no light would rise over the earth without the sun, so too without the priesthood no more grace or holiness would come to us in the Church. The sun pours out its luminous rays on the world; the priesthood works in all souls, lavishly bestows its gifts, and spreads over everyone the perfume of its holiness. The purpose for which Christ instituted it was that the Church might receive from it all her sanctification, all her beauty, all her splendor."[2]

---

[1] John Chrysostom, *On the Priesthood* VI, 2, 8-9.

[2] *La Tradition sacerdotale: études sur le sacerdoce*, Bibliothèque de la faculté catholique de théologie de Lyon, vol. 7 (Le Puy: Éditions Xavier Mappus, 1959), see 170-171.

Plainly the holiness that should shine in the priest comes from God's holiness. Priests must become perfect and holy after the likeness of Jesus Christ. And so, as priests, we must work to acquire all the human and Christian virtues with a view to being really configured to Christ and resembling Him. Indeed, Saint Gregory of Nyssa exhorts us:

> When we consider that Christ is the true light, having nothing in common with deceit, we learn that our own life also must shine with the rays of that Truth. Now these rays of the Sun of Justice are the virtues which pour out to enlighten us so that we may "put away the works of darkness and walk honorably as in broad daylight." When we reject the deeds of darkness and do everything in the light of day, we become light and, as light should, we give light to others by our actions. If we truly think of Christ as our source of holiness, we shall refrain from anything wicked or impure in thought or act and thus show ourselves to be worthy bearers of his Name. For the quality of holiness is shown not by what we say but by what we do in life.[3]

This is the situation with the priesthood. Christ Jesus gave us a very beautiful, luminous, and clear icon of His priestly being: the Sacrament of Holy Orders is this icon of Jesus, the High Priest. But our compromises with the world have added layers of mediocre-quality paint on the divine work of art. The work has lost its brilliance. It is therefore advisable to restore it, and to do that, we must strip away these additions so as to rediscover the original. Benedict

---

[3] Gregory of Nyssa, *Treatise on Christian Perfection*, cited in *The Liturgy of the Hours* (New York: Catholic Book Publishing, 1975), IV:107–108.

XVI and I had intended to invite priests to this work of reform, of return to the form intended by God, in publishing *From the Depths of Our Hearts*.[4] In this book, each of us had opened up paths toward a restoration of a fully sacerdotal way of life for priests. Some of its proposals were daring. Unfortunately, many people remembered only the most polemical and most political interpretations of those lines. Nevertheless, the book found an attentive, benevolent reader in the person of Pope Francis, who has unceasingly invited priests to renew their deepest being. In asking us to break with self-referentiality, the pope invites us to rediscover a priesthood that does not refer to itself but is an icon of Christ the Priest.

How is this restoration to be carried out? How can the accumulated layers of paint and varnish be stripped off? In this book, I propose to you a simple method: Let the Church speak! Let Her saints and Her Doctors speak. Let us espouse their way of looking at things so as to renew our perspectives.

I wanted a simple, short book that would be accessible to everyone. I wanted a book that would help priests rediscover their profound identity and help the people of God to renew their way of looking at priests.

I will let the saints speak: men and women, laymen and clerics. Their purity of soul will enable us to find again the essence of the priesthood. Do not look for a treatise of academic theology in their words. The theology of the saints is on display here. It is contemplative and spiritual but also practical and concrete. I will let the Church speak in Her Magisterium, because through Her, the voice of Christ comes to us.

---

[4] Benedict XVI and Robert Cardinal Sarah, *From the Depths of Our Hearts: Priesthood, Celibacy, and the Crisis of the Catholic Church*, trans. Michael J. Miller (San Francisco: Ignatius Press, 2020).

Each text will be for us like a renewed way of looking, a luminous feature to draw more accurately the spiritual portrait of the priest as Jesus Christ intended him and as we need him today. In light of these teachings of the Church and of the saints, together, we will examine the quality of our relations with God. We will try to realize that those who serve God and the Altar must no longer get mixed up in the despicable acts of the earth. We will try to put Psalm 16 into practice concretely: "The LORD is my chosen portion and my cup; you hold my lot. The lines have fallen for me in pleasant places; yes, I have a goodly heritage" (Ps 16:5-6).

With you, I observe the storm that is violently shaking the Church: major upheavals, disturbing challenges in doctrinal and liturgical matters, the collapse of Catholic moral theology, the omnipresence of evil in the world, leaving the Church defenseless against the far-reaching changes in society. These things trouble us and deeply sadden us all. Our priestly identity, tarnished by a minority of the clergy, is vehemently disputed. One current of thought denies the essential difference between the ministerial priesthood and the common priesthood of the baptized. They would like to assign to all Catholics the ministerial functions above and beyond those for which the sacraments of Baptism and Confirmation would qualify them. By starting out from this purely functional and sociological concept of the Sacrament of Holy Orders, do we not run the risk of completely distorting the priesthood of the New Covenant?

This sociological view of the priesthood has given rise to pressures and demands for the ordination of women and of married men. However, Pope John Paul II, in his Apostolic Letter *Mulieris dignitatem* (August 15, 1988), had clearly stated and explained the close connection between Christ's spousal relation to the Church and the fact that ordination is reserved to men.

Here are his unforgettable words:

We find ourselves at the very heart of the Paschal Mystery, which completely reveals the spousal love of God. Christ is the Bridegroom because "he has given himself": his body has been "given," his blood has been "poured out (cf. Lk 22:19-20). In this way "he loved them to the end" (Jn 13:1). The "sincere gift" contained in the sacrifice of the Cross gives definitive prominence to the spousal meaning of God's love. As the Redeemer of the world, Christ is the Bridegroom of the Church. *The Eucharist is the Sacrament of our Redemption.* It is *the Sacrament of the Bridegroom and of the Bride.* The Eucharist makes present and realizes anew in a sacramental manner the redemptive act of Christ, who "creates" the Church, his body. Christ is united with this "body" as the bridegroom with the bride. All this is contained in the Letter to the Ephesians. The perennial "unity of the two" that exists between man and woman from the very "beginning" is introduced into this "great mystery" of Christ and of the Church. Since Christ, in instituting the Eucharist, linked it in such an explicit way to the priestly service of the Apostles, it is legitimate to conclude that he thereby wished to express the relationship between man and woman, between what is "feminine" and what is "masculine." It is a relationship willed by God both in the mystery of creation and in the mystery of Redemption. It is *the Eucharist* above all that expresses *the redemptive act of Christ the Bridegroom towards the Church the Bride.* This is clear and unambiguous when the sacramental ministry of the Eucharist, in which the priest acts "*in persona Christi*," is performed by a man. This explanation confirms the teaching of the Declaration *Inter Insigniores* (October 15, 1976), published at the behest of Paul VI in response to the question concerning the admission of women to the ministerial priesthood. [*MD* 26].

Moreover, we live today in the middle of a godless world. In Western society the silent apostasy of man who believes that he is happier without God is making great strides. In this arid desert, I invite you to become more and more clearly obvious signs of the presence of God in the world. I invite you to sit often at the feet of Jesus to listen to Him speak to us about the Father's infinite love and to relearn from Him the primary and fundamental task that the Lord entrusts to us. Western society killed God, and this is why it is decadent and is slowly euthanatizing itself, despite all appearances of material prosperity. With the death of God, intellectuals thought that they would achieve autonomy and total human freedom. But the death of God led, in fact, to the death of freedom and obscured a correct concept of the human being. God is the one and only compass that can orient us toward happiness.

As Benedict XVI often repeats, God became man for us. His human creation is so dear to His heart that He united Himself to it and thus integrated Himself into its history in a very concrete way. He speaks with us. He lives with us, works with us, suffers with us, and hears our cries of anguish. He took death upon Himself in order to save us from death and sin. Often theology mentions this with words that are too erudite, incomprehensible and inaccessible. This is precisely how we run the risk of becoming specialists in God, masters of the Faith, instead of allowing ourselves to be transformed, renewed, governed, and divinized by it. The way in which we must restore to God His place in the world is by our lives and our witness, entirely imbued by the Gospel.

This book is an invitation to sit at the feet of Jesus, our High Priest, so as to allow ourselves to be renewed in our priesthood. At His feet and following in His footsteps, we learn to be priests, to let ourselves be formed in His image and likeness, and to enter fully into the Christian mysteries that we celebrate with faith.

Jesus teaches us that through His priesthood, God our Father started a love story with us, an infinite and demanding love that goes even to death. He wishes to associate all of creation with it. The only possible counterbalance against the evil that threatens us is our total abandonment to this Love. This is the true counterbalance against evil. The power of evil springs from our refusal to love God.

The one and only objective of these lines is to open our hearts to listen again to Jesus, who prays for us priests:

> Father,... I do not pray that you should take them out of the world, but that you should keep them from the evil one. They are not of the world, even as I am not of the world. Sanctify them in the truth; your word is truth. As you sent me into the world, so I have sent them into the world. And for their sake I consecrate myself, that they also may be consecrated in truth. (Jn 17:1, 15–19)

Their purpose of these lines is to encourage you to be steadfast and faithful to the grace of your priesthood, whatever trials, sufferings, tribulations, and insults you may have to endure for the Name of the Lord Jesus.

Their purpose is to remind you that Christ's Passion is a permanent reality inherent in the life of a priest. The Carthusians teach us this: *Stat Crux dum volvitur orbis*, the Cross alone stands still while the world turns around it. Christ suffers and dies even today through His priests and faithful Christians.

For Eternity

This book is meant to lead you, following Saint Francis of Assisi, to a profound conversion, so as to bear, as he did, the stigmata of Christ in your own body and, in his words, to take as your rule of life "the decision to follow in its entirety the Holy Gospel of Our Lord Jesus Christ."

I

Toward a Reform of the Clergy

Based on a meditation by Saint Catherine of Siena

————— ⟨∞⟩ —————

Introduction

I like to reread regularly the writings of Saint Catherine of Siena. Such a vehement love for Christ and for the Church dwells in the soul of this daughter of Saint Dominic that she wakes us from our slumber and denounces our lukewarmness and our compromises with sin. This woman knows how to talk to priests. How freely she speaks! Who would dare to say such things today? No one will ever convince me that this saint was unable to take her full place as a woman in the Church. She had very little education yet did not hesitate to threaten priests and bishops, not in order to demand some sort of flattened, undifferentiated equality between men and women, or to claim titles or her right to be a deaconess or a priestess, but to call each one to be fully what he is: a living member of the Mystical Body of Christ. Therefore, she does not hesitate to declare that the misfortunes of the Church are caused by the lukewarmness and sins of the clergy. She does not hesitate to call for a reform of the pastors. And what is this reform? Is it a transformation of the priesthood, a recasting of the Sacrament of

Holy Orders? On the contrary, it is the conversion of priests to a life consistent with their sacramental state.

Allow me to make a reflection inspired by these lines by Catherine of Siena. I sometimes wonder about the apparent failure of the great missionary movement initiated in the nineteenth century. So much holiness, so much generosity, so many priests making enormous sacrifices to proclaim the gospel to all nations! I think with gratitude about the missionaries who were willing to visit the smallest of the most remote villages. Thanks to them, I, too, know Christ today. Then this movement seemed to wear out and dry up. It is as though Christian Europe got tired of it. The great movement of conversions and baptisms would have slowed in Africa and Asia had it not been for the magnificent flourishing of the local churches and the many vocations to the priestly and religious life that God raised up in the mission territories. What happened? As we discover today so many cases of pedophilia, we can perhaps answer that question. How could we be fruitful, if such sins were hidden in our midst? How could our Church be missionary if, among her priests, some individuals continued in this way to tarnish and soil the pure, holy work of so many others? The words of Catherine of Siena resound with current relevance: "What gives life is for them a cause of death because they abuse the blood of the Son of God."

My brother priests, have we abused the blood of Christ? Have we abused the sacraments? Have we celebrated with joyful fear and loving respect the mystery of Christ's Precious Blood? During our Eucharistic liturgies, have we given God the primacy? Are our liturgical celebrations moments of adoration and glorification of the divine majesty, or have they become the community's celebration of itself or ethnic and cultural displays? Have we administered the sacraments inattentively? Have we neglected the Sacrament of Penance in which this blood washes our sins away?

My brother priests, have we abused this milk of doctrine? Have we not sullied it with many external impurities and compromises? I make my examination of conscience with you. Or rather, I let this young woman from Siena interrogate me from her place in the fourteenth century. Yes, let her call us into question. Let Catherine's words restore for us the meaning of sin and revive in us a dramatic and tragic awareness of the refusal of God. Sin, our sin as priests, is not a minor detail. It cost the blood of God Incarnate. Our reform, our return to Him, is the fruit of this blood and the condition for the health of the entire Church. For we are the cause of her sick state. Saint Catherine—the woman who publicly intervened in the life of the Church by asking Pope Gregory XI to leave Avignon to return to the See of Peter—is buried in Rome. By dint of her cries, threats, prayers, and love, she finally succeeded in dragging the Vicar of Christ to Rome. Her body is visible beneath the main altar in the Basilica of Saint Mary above Minerva. She is there, lying beneath the table of sacrifice where, every day, the blood flows that waters our souls and makes the Church alive. She calls to us and reminds us of our vocation as priests and of our mission in the world. Her body, which rests among us, is a permanent questioning.

Have we not become worldly, secularized, and tepid? Are we not being towed by the world—a materialistic, atheistic world? Left on our own and often disoriented by some pastors themselves, we feel lost, intimidated, and discouraged by the powers of this world. Let us not lose hope. Let us stand firm in our faith in the Lord Jesus Christ. Saint John reassures us when he writes in his First Letter: "Who is it that overcomes the world but he who believes that Jesus is the Son of God?" (1 Jn 5:5).

We must not let go of any of our zeal for Catholic truth; we should remember that the situation of the early Church was not much different from ours. Nevertheless, a handful of fishermen from Galilee, who "were uneducated, common men" (Acts 4:13), powerless in worldly affairs but full of faith, conquered the whole world. Henri de Lubac says:

> The Church is not only the first of the works of the sanctifying Spirit, but also that which includes, conditions, and absorbs all the rest. The entire process of salvation is worked out in her.... Existing as she does by the will of God, the Church is necessary to us—necessary as a means. And more than this. The mystery of the Church is all Mystery in miniature; it is our own mystery par excellence. It lays hold on the whole of us. It surrounds us on all sides, for it is in his Church that God looks upon us and loves us, in her that he desires us and we encounter him, and in her that we cleave to him and are made blessed by him.[5]

It is impossible for us to understand the priesthood apart from the Catholic Church. Any reform of the clergy must start with a profound look at the Church in faith, because in Her all the sacraments of the New Covenant are generated and we ourselves become disciples of Jesus Christ.

But the Church, the whole Church, the only Church, today's as well as the Church of yesterday and of tomorrow, is the sacrament of Jesus Christ. She is nothing else. For many of our contemporaries, and even among Her own children, however, the Church appears as a merely human structure at the service of society. Nowadays people can see in the Church only Her human merits: She is highly esteemed only when She employs Her resources for a

---

[5] Henri de Lubac, *The Splendor of the Church*, trans. Michael Mason (San Francisco: Ignatius Press, 1986, 1999), 45–46.

temporal end, such as relieving poverty or welcoming migrants. She is appreciated for Her advocacy on behalf of ecology, for fighting politically on behalf of peace, justice, and fraternity among peoples.

We observe today, within the Church, major internal struggles and doctrinal divisions. Even the synods of Bishops, which were designed as an encounter for pastoral exchange and to share our common mission, have turned into a battlefield where groups confront each other, each one trying to impose his theological, moral, or ideological position by force. As Henri de Lubac puts it:

> The quarrels of the Church's own children do not merely weaken the Church; they disfigure her in the eyes of the world and demolish her from within.... For my own part I will go so far as to say that if the Church were not what she claims to be—if she did not, essentially, live by faith in Jesus Christ, the faith proclaimed by Peter on the road to Caesarea, I should not wait for her to disappoint me at the human level before I separated from her. For in that case, all her benefits on the human level, all her splendor, all the riches of her history, all her promise for the future could not make up for the dreadful void at the heart of her. The hypothesis is of course not merely false but impossible; yet were things so, all those good things would be the garish trappings of an imposture, and the hope planted by her in our hearts would be a deception, and we should be "of all men most miserable" (1 Cor 15:14–19). If Christ is not her wealth, the Church is certainly destitute; if the Spirit of Christ does not flourish in her, she is certainly sterile. If Christ is not her Architect and Cornerstone, and his Spirit is not the mortar that binds together the living stones of which she is built, then her building is indeed fallen into

ruin. If she does not reflect the unique beauty of the face of Christ, the Church is without beauty....[6] The knowledge on which she prides herself is false, and the wisdom that is her ornament is false, unless both are summed up in Jesus Christ; if her light does not come wholly from Jesus Christ, she certainly has us captive in the shadow of death. All her teaching is a lie if she does not announce the Truth which is Jesus Christ; all her glory is vanity if she does not find it in the humility of Jesus Christ. Her very name is something foreign to us if it does not at once call to mind the one Name given to men for their salvation (see Acts 4:12). If she is not the sacrament, the effective sign, of Jesus Christ, then she is nothing.

The Church's unique mission is that of making him present to men. She is to announce him, show him, and give him, to all; the rest, I repeat, is a superabundance. We know that she cannot fail in this mission; she is, and always will be truly, the Church of Christ—"I am with you all days, even unto the consummation of the world" (Mt 28:20). But she should also be in her members what she is in herself; she should be *through* us what she is *for* us. Jesus Christ should continue to be proclaimed through us and to appear through us. That is something more than an obligation; we may go so far as to say that it is an organic necessity. The question is, do the facts always answer to it? Does the Church truly announce Jesus Christ through our ministry?[7]

I ask you the question. It is a vital one.

[6] Augustine, *Sermo* 44, 2.
[7] De Lubac, *The Splendor of the Church*, 217–220, emended.

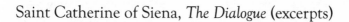

Saint Catherine of Siena, *The Dialogue* (excerpts)

God promises that the sufferings of his servants
will be rewarded with rest and the reform of the Church

I tell you further: The more the mystic body of holy Church is filled with troubles now, the more it will abound in delight and consolation. And this shall be its delight: the reform of good holy shepherds who are flowers of glory, who praise and glorify my name, offering me the fragrance of virtue rooted in truth. This is the reform of the fragrant blossoming of my ministers and shepherds—not that the fruit of this bride needs to be reformed, because it never spoils or is diminished by the sins of its ministers. So be glad, you and your spiritual father and my other servants, in your bitterness. For I, eternal Truth, promise to refresh you, and after your bitterness I will give you consolation, along with great suffering, in the reform of holy Church.[8]

God complains about the sins of Christians,
particularly those of His ministers

God let himself be forced by her tears and chained by her holy
desire. And turning to her with a glance at once full of mercy and
of sadness he said:

Dearest daughter, because your tears are joined to my charity and are shed for love of me, your weeping has power over me and the pain in your desires binds me like a chain. But

---

[8] *Catherine of Siena: The Dialogue*, trans. Suzanne Noffke, O.P. (Mahwah, NJ: Paulist Press, 1980), 47.

look how my bride has disfigured her face! She is leprous
with impurity and selfishness. Her breasts are swollen
because of the pride and avarice of those who feed there:
the universal body of Christianity and the mystic body of
holy Church. I am speaking of my ministers who feed at her
breasts. They ought not only to feed themselves, but hold
to those breasts the whole body of Christianity as well as
whoever would rise from the darkness of unbelief and be
bound into the body of my Church.

Do you see then how ignorantly and blindly they serve
out the marvelous milk and blood of this bride—how
thanklessly and with what filthy hands? And do you see
with what presumption and lack of reverence it is received?
And so the precious life-giving blood of my only-begotten
Son, which dispelled death and darkness, confounded
falsehood, and brought the gift of light and truth, all
too often, because of their sinfulness, brings them death
instead.

For those who are receptive this blood bestowed and
accomplished all that they need to be saved and made perfect. But since its gift of life and grace is in proportion to
the soul's readiness and desire, it deals death to the wicked.
So it gives death rather than life to those who receive it
unworthily, in the darkness of deadly sin. The fault for
this is not in the blood. Nor does it lie in the ministers.
The latter may be just as evil or worse, but their sin cannot spoil or contaminate the blood or lessen its grace and
power, nor can it harm those they serve. They are, however,
bringing on themselves the evil of sin, which will certainly
be punished unless they set themselves right through true
contrition and contempt for sin.

Those who receive the blood unworthily then, I repeat, are harmed not through any fault in the blood nor because of any fault on the ministers' part, but because of their own evil disposition and their own sin. For they have defiled their minds and bodies with such wretched filth, and have been so cruel to themselves and to their neighbors. They have cruelly deprived themselves of grace, willfully trampling underfoot the fruit of the blood, since it was by virtue of the blood that they were freed in holy baptism from the taint of original sin.... This is why I gave the Word, my only-begotten Son. The clay of humankind was spoiled by the sin of the first man, Adam, and so all of you, as vessels made from that clay, were spoiled and unfit to hold eternal life.[9]

Many other sins committed by bad pastors

How I detest this!... Their bride is not the breviary (indeed, they have treated this bride, the breviary, like an adulteress) but a wretched she-devil who indecently lives with them....

O wretched man! What has become of you? You ought to be hunting souls for the glory and praise of my name in the garden of holy Church, and you are going about in the woods! But because you have become a beast, you harbor within your soul the animals of so many deadly sins. This is why you have become a trapper and fowler of beasts: because the orchard of your soul has become a wild tangle of brambles. That is why you have found your pleasure in wandering through deserted places looking for wild beasts.

[9] *Dialogue,* 50–51.

Blush for shame and look at your sins, for wherever you turn you have reason to be ashamed. But you are not ashamed, because you have lost all true and holy fear of me. Like a shameless whore you boast about your exalted position in the world and your fine family and your brigade of children. And if you have no children you are trying to have some so as to have heirs to leave behind. But you are a thieving bandit, because you know very well that your heirs are supposed to be none other than the poor and holy Church. O devil incarnate! Without any light you seek what you ought not to be seeking; you boast and brag about what ought to deeply confound you and make you ashamed in my presence (for I see your inmost heart) and in the presence of all creation. You are confused, but the horns of your pride keep you from seeing your confusion.

O dearest daughter, I set them on the bridge on my Truth's teaching to serve you pilgrims with the sacraments of holy Church, and they are instead in the wretched river beneath the bridge, and there in the river of worldly pleasures and baseness they exercise their ministry. They are not even aware that the wave of death is upon them and that they are being carried along together with their lords the devils whose servants they have been and whom they have allowed to guide them along the path of the river without any anchor-hold. Unless they change their ways they will be swept on to eternal damnation with such reproach that your tongue could never describe it. And it will be much worse for them as priests than for seculars. The very same sin is punished more severely in them than in others whose calling was in the world. And their enemies will rise up to accuse them more reproachfully at the moment of death.[10]

The difference between the death of the just and that of sinners;
First the death of the just

Their dignity is greater in virtue of their priesthood because I have directly entrusted to them the task of feeding souls for my honor. Although all of you have the duty of warmly loving your neighbors, to my priests is entrusted the ministry of the blood and the care of souls, and if they do this conscientiously with love for virtue they receive more than others do.

Oh, how blissful are [the] souls [of these priests] when they reach the moment of death! Because they proclaimed and defended the faith for their neighbors, it has become incarnate for them in the marrow of their souls. It is with this faith that they see their place in Me.

They lived in hope, trusting in My providence and not at all in themselves or in their own knowledge. And because they ceased trusting in themselves they were not inordinately attached to any created person or thing and so lived in voluntary poverty. Therefore [at the moment of death], this hope of theirs reaches out toward me with great joy.

Their hearts were vessels of affection that carried My name. They proclaimed it with burning love, both by the example of their good and holy living and by their teaching of the word to their neighbors. So now this heart of theirs rises up with unspeakable love and with this thrust of love

---

[10] *Dialogue*, 261–262.

seizes Me, its goal. It brings to Me the pearl of justice, which it had always kept in sight by being just to everyone and doing its duty with discernment. Therefore it offers Me the justice of true humility and glory and praise for My name in thanks to Me for the grace to have run its course with a pure and holy conscience. And for itself it has the justice that it deserves, while professing itself unworthy to have received and still be receiving such grace.

Their conscience bears them good witness to Me, and in justice I reward it with the crown of justice adorned with pearls of virtue, that is, the fruit their charity has drawn from the virtues.

O earthly angel! Blessed are you that you have not been ungrateful for the benefits you have received from Me, and that you have not been guilty of negligence or foolishness. Conscientiously and with true light you kept your eyes on your subjects, and as a faithful, courageous shepherd you followed the teaching of the true good shepherd, the gentle Christ Jesus, My only-begotten Son. This is why you are now passing through Him [the gate] so regally, immersed and bathed in his blood, with your herd of little sheep. For by your holy teaching and life you have led many of them to everlasting life, preserved many of them in grace.

O dearest daughter, the sight of devils cannot harm these souls. Because of the sight of Me, which they see in faith and possess in love, and because there is none of the venom of sin in them, this darksome terror can neither harm nor frighten them. They have no slavish fear but only holy fear. So they are not afraid of the devil's delusions; because of the supernatural light of Holy Scripture, they recognize them for what they are and they suffer neither darkness nor spiritual distress from them.

Thus gloriously they pass, bathed in the blood, hungering for the salvation of souls, all ablaze with charity for their neighbors, coming through the gate of the Word and entering into me. And My goodness assigns them their places, measuring out to all according to the measure of loving charity they have brought to Me.[11]

Meditation

Whatever difficulties the Church may be going through these days, whatever horrible scandals some high-ranking prelates have been guilty of, whatever corrupt financial deals the Church has been accused of: dear priests and dear lay faithful, let us never entertain the fatal idea of "breaking the bond of peace by a sacrilegious separation from our Mother, Holy Church." Let us not flatter ourselves that, while putting ourselves outside the Church, we can still remain in fellowship with Christ. Rather, let us remind ourselves with Saint Augustine: "In order to live by the Spirit of Christ, it is necessary to remain in his Body, and we have the Holy Spirit within us to the extent that we love the Church of Christ."[12] It may be that many things in the human context of the Church disappoint us. It can also happen that, without any fault of our own, we may be profoundly misunderstood. Maybe we have to undergo persecutions even within the Church. Let us be happy, however, in the presence of the Father, Who sees in secret, to participate this

[11] *Dialogue*, 265–266.
[12] See Augustine, *Homilies on the Gospel of John*, tract. 32, no. 8.

way in the "*veritatis unitas*," "unity of truth," which we implore for everyone on Good Friday. Let us be happy if we purchase, then, at the price of the soul's blood this intimate experience that will make our words effective when we have to support a weakened brother, telling him with Saint John Chrysostom: "Do not separate from the Church at all! No power has strength as great as hers. Your hope is the Church. Your salvation is the Church. Your refuge is the Church. She is higher than the heavens and wider than the earth. She never ages. Her vigor is eternal."[13]

To dispel all discouragement and every whim of breaking with the Church, let us take two examples: Martin Luther and Saint Francis of Assisi. By way of an introduction, let us look at what Georges Bernanos says on this subject: the great French Catholic writer contrasts the reformer's attitude with the resistance of the saints. In a work titled *Brother Martin*, we find this very enlightening reflection:

> There are Pharisees in the Church, Pharisaism continues to circulate in the veins of this great Body, and every time charity grows weak in it, the chronic infection leads to a severe crisis.... Indignation has never redeemed anyone, but it has probably lost many souls, and all the simoniacal bacchanalia of sixteenth-century Rome would not have been such a windfall for the devil had they not struck the decisive blow of casting Luther into despair, and two-thirds of sorrowful Christendom along with that indomitable monk. Luther and his followers despaired of the Church, and anyone who despairs of the Church sooner or later runs the risk of despairing of man. From this perspective Protestantism appears to me as a compromise with despair....

[13] John Chrysostom, *Homily on Eutropius* 6; PG 53, 402.

Martin Luther's misfortune was the claim to reform.... [Now,] whoever pretends to reform the Church ... with the same means used to reform temporal society not only will fail in his undertaking but will inevitably end up finding himself outside the Church.... The only way to reform the Church is to suffer for her. The only way to reform the visible Church is to suffer for the invisible Church. The only way to reform the vices of the Church is to lavish on her the example of one's own most heroic virtues. It is quite possible that Saint Francis of Assisi found the debauchery and simony of the prelates no less revolting than Luther did. Indeed, he certainly suffered more cruelly because of it, since his nature was quite different from that of the monk from Wittenberg. Yet Francis did not challenge iniquity; he was not tempted to confront it. He threw himself into poverty, immersing himself in it as deeply as possible along with his followers. For them it was the source of all absolution and all purity. Instead of attempting to snatch from the Church her ill-gotten goods, he lavished invisible treasures on her, and under this beggar's gentle hand the heap of gold and lust began to blossom like a hedge in April.... The Church does not need reformers but saints.[14]

Let us speak first of all about the reformer Martin Luther. In 2017, we commemorated the five-hundredth anniversary of the day when the Augustinian monk posted on a church door in Wittenberg ninety-five theses that condemned, in particular, the practice of indulgences as the Church teaches it but also other

---

[14] Georges Bernanos, "Frère Martin," in *La Vocation spirituelle de la France*, unpublished works collected and presented by Jean-Loup Bernanos (Paris: Plon, 1975).

points concerning the Faith, such as the reality of Purgatory. This public act is usually considered the start of what is commonly called the "Reformation." As of 1517, in reality, and despite the vicissitudes that would follow, Martin Luther had already broken with the Church of Christ in his heart, and from then on, he followed only his erroneous personal views. As we will see, however, before that, Martin Luther was a pious, zealous monk.

Born in 1483 into a good Christian family, Martin was attracted at a very early age by religion and, later on, by theology. Whereas his father hoped that he would become a lawyer, he decided to become an Augustinian monk, entering that order in 1505. After being ordained a priest in 1507, he earned a doctorate in theology in 1512. From then on, his life would be that of a teacher and a preacher. Luther had received a good formation, and he certainly had been influenced on the intellectual level by his reading of several great authors, whether Aristotle or William of Ockham. However, on the basis of his personal interior life, his intimate spiritual experience, Luther would construct a new doctrine that would stray from the teaching of the Catholic Church. Moreover, he was endowed with a strong, passionate temperament, and as a corollary, he experienced strong temptations to gluttony and against chastity, and he had a propensity for anger and a prideful spirit of independence. In 1515, within the framework of his teaching, he started to comment on the letters of Saint Paul, in particular, the first of them in the biblical sequence, the Letter to the Romans, which is immensely rich, incredibly brilliant, but also formidably difficult to understand. Based on what he thought he understood of this text, relying solely on his thought and without referring to Church Tradition, Martin Luther elaborated a new theology that, from then on, was radically incompatible with that of the Catholic Church, even though the external, public rupture would take a while. The question that tormented him was this: "Can I be saved while I still feel my temptations?"

According to Catholic doctrine, thanks to Christ's merits, someone who accepts divine revelation by faith and, moved by the hope of divine salvation, wants to repent of his sins and turn to God, obtains the forgiveness of his sins through grace and obtains the regeneration and sanctification of his soul; he then becomes, as Saint Peter puts it, a "partaker of the divine nature" (2 Pet 1:4). Saint Cyril of Alexandria says: "Indeed, illuminated by the only Son, we are transformed into this Word that gives life to all beings."[15] Saint Paul, in his Letter to the Ephesians, declares, "Out of the great love with which [God] loved us, even when we were dead through our trespasses, [he] made us alive together with Christ (by grace you have been saved)" (Eph 2:4-5). The Christian who lives by charity is therefore, as Saint Paul often says, a "saint," because he has been interiorly purified, transformed, sanctified, and he has really become a Friend of God by an effective, permanent likeness. Being a Friend of God, he spontaneously does the works of God, the good works of virtue that merit salvation for him, through Christ's grace present in him, and therefore the happiness of Heaven.

Luther rejects this truth. For him, the fact of having embraced the Faith and the Christian life does not take sin away from the soul. For Martin Luther, the Christian remains, in reality, still a sinner, and his soul remains altogether corrupt. But since Christ merited salvation for mankind through the sacrifice of the Cross, the cloak of Christ's merits covers over the filth of my soul, and our Father, seeing this cloak on me, accepts me into Heaven. Good

---

[15] Cyril of Alexandria, *Commentary on the Second Letter to the Corinthians*.

works, therefore, have no power to merit, since man still remains a sinner interiorly, but they simply encourage the Christian to persevere in faith.

This is the heart of what Luther calls "the truth of the Gospel." From it, the rest of his doctrine follows naturally: in the first place, his questioning of the institutional Church. He says that She is not divine, if only because She claims that man can be saved by good works, whereas, as Luther's disappointing experience in monastic life showed, these good works are incapable of removing sin. Since the Christian's soul is not transformed by grace, the sacraments no longer work any real change in it. For the same reason, Holy Mass loses all meaning. He would keep only a memorial of the Last Supper, to remind us about the unique sacrifice of Christ on the Cross and to revive our faith in His redemption. Nevertheless, Luther was not content to set the Mass aside. As a priest in an irregular situation and a monk unfaithful to his vows, he developed a hatred for the Holy Sacrifice of the Mass: "The Mass," he declared in 1521, "is the greatest and the most horrible of the papist abominations." And he concluded: "If the Mass falls, the papacy collapses." Since good works, particularly monastic vows, were useless and deceptive, Luther decided to return to the lay state, and in 1525, he married a former nun, Catherine of Bora, with whom he would have six children. When Martin Luther died on February 18, 1546, the Thirty Years' War was ravaging Germany, a war that extended to almost all of Europe and then to the whole world.

Martin Luther the reformer therefore failed: instead of purifying the Church from within, he tore the Mystical Body of Christ, causing terrible wars of religion.[16] But God governs the world through

[16] See Jacques Maritain, *Three Reformers: Luther, Descartes, Rousseau* (New York: Charles Scribner's Sons, 1929).

what we call Providence. When the Church excommunicated Martin Luther in 1521, God raised up that same year Saint Ignatius of Loyola, who, by his preparatory schools for young men and his *Spiritual Exercises*, would try to restore the soul of the Church and help Christian civilization survive.

As we will see, the situation was quite different with Francis of Assisi, who, in the thirteenth century, undertook to reform the Church by way of sanctity and penance.[17] In order to understand Saint Francis's way of reforming, we must start with conversion—and concretely from what is called "kissing the leper." The saint himself testifies to it in these terms: "During the time when I was still in my sins, the sight of a leper was unbearable to me. But the Lord himself led me among them; I cared for them with all my heart; and in return, what had seemed to me so bitter had changed for me into sweetness for the soul and for the body. Then I waited a little while, and I said farewell to the world."[18]

Jesus tells us: "If any man would come after me, let him deny himself and take up his cross and follow me. For whoever would save his life will lose it, and whoever loses his life for my sake will find it" (Mt 16:24-25). Francis of Assisi, in kissing the leper, renounced himself by accepting what was most "bitter" and what was most repugnant to his nature. He did himself violence. Francis did not go spontaneously to be with the lepers, driven by some human compassion. "The Lord himself led me among them," he writes. Father Raniero Cantalamessa points out: "Francis did not espouse poverty or even the poor; he espoused Christ, and it was

---

[17] See Raniero Cantalamessa, First Advent Homily at the Vatican, December 6, 2013.

[18] Excerpt from the *Testament* of Saint Francis of Assisi, 1-3, quoted in Cantalamessa, First Advent Homily.

for love of Him that he espoused Lady Poverty 'in a second wedding,' so to speak. It will always be so in 'Christian holiness.' "[19] How could such an intimate and personal event as the conversion of young Francis unleash a movement that would change the face of the Church in his day and at the same time exert such a strong influence on history down to our day?

We must look for a moment at the situation then. In Francis's time, everyone was more or less aware that the Church needed to be reformed. The Body of the Church was experiencing tensions and deep rifts. The Church was collapsing and falling into ruin under the weight of Her infidelities and corruption, Her worldly behavior, Her luxury, and Her sins. We are acquainted with these two very significant episodes from the life of Saint Francis: first, the famous words from the crucifix in the Church of San Damiano: "Go, Francis, and repair my Church which, as you see, is falling into ruin"; and then the dream of Pope Innocent III, in which he saw Francis supporting on his shoulders the Cathedral Basilica of Saint John Lateran that was collapsing.

We can describe Francis's way of reform with this simple expression: a radical return to the Gospel. During a Mass, Francis heard the Gospel passage about the sending of the disciples: Jesus "sent them out to preach the kingdom of God and to heal. And he said to them, 'Take nothing for your journey, no staff, nor bag, nor bread, nor money; and do not have two tunics'" (Lk 9:2-3). This was for him a dazzling revelation, the kind that transforms and orients a whole lifetime. From that day on, his mission appeared clear to him; a simple and radical return to the true Gospel that was lived and preached by Jesus. Concretely it was a matter of

---

[19] Excerpt from the *Testament* of Saint Francis of Assisi, 1-3, quoted in Cantalamessa, First Advent Homily.

reviving in the world the way of life led by Jesus and the Apostles, as described in the Gospels. Saint Francis started his Rule by saying this to his friars: "The Rule and the life of the Friars Minor is this: to observe the Holy Gospel of Our Lord Jesus Christ." This radical return to the Gospel is reflected above all in Francis's preaching. It is surprising, but he almost always speaks about "doing penance." From his conversion on, with great fervor and joy, he preached repentance and edified everyone by the simplicity and purity of his words and the magnificence of his heart. Everywhere he went, Francis told, urged, and begged people to do penance. Is this not the message that the Blessed Virgin Mary repeats to us in each of her apparitions: "Pray and do penance"? For no evangelization is possible without the practice of repentance. Francis just revived the great call to conversion with which the preaching of Jesus commenced in the Gospel and that of the Apostles on the day of Pentecost. He did not have to explain what he meant by "conversion": his whole life showed it. This is the way of holiness, which, within the Church, regenerates her in depth by cleansing her from her sins. However, following the example of the saints, we must pray, pray, pray, and do penance.

II

A Remedy for Hypocrisy

Based on a meditation by Saint Gregory the Great

Introduction

The priest makes Christ sacramentally present. What an unfathomable mystery! Even if the priest is a liar, a pervert, a mediocrity, and the vilest, most repugnant of sinners, Christ's hand would still bless, sanctify, absolve, and consecrate through him. Saint Augustine sums this up in very strong language by comparing the priest to the traitor Judas: "When the Apostle Peter baptizes, Jesus is the one who baptizes in him, but when Judas the traitor baptizes, Jesus is still the one who baptizes in him."[20] What a mystery! The challenge in the life of a priest, therefore, is to become day by day what he is in the depths of his soul. He constantly seeks to be conformed to Christ, Whose minister he is. All the movements of his heart, his conduct, his thoughts, his actions, and his words will have only one concern: to reproduce the mysteries of the life of Jesus. We Christians have died with Christ; we are "always carrying in the body the death of Jesus, so that the life of Jesus may also be manifested

---

[20] Augustine, *Homilies on the Epistle of John* VI, 7.

in our bodies" (2 Cor 4:10). Therefore, we no longer live our own lives but live the life of Christ, "a life of innocence, a life of purity and holiness, a life of simplicity and all the virtues," Saint Ambrose says. Thus, every priest, by his consecration and his mission, truly has a personal duty to carry the death of Jesus and to reproduce, in his life, the life and holiness of Christ. Saint John Paul II declares:

> We see precisely in the Curé of Ars a priest who was not content to perform redemptive actions externally; he took part in them in his very being, in his love for Christ, in his constant prayer, in offering up his trials or his voluntary mortifications. I said this already to the priests of Notre-Dame in Paris on May 30, 1980: "The Curé of Ars remains for all the countries of the world a peerless model, both of the performance of the priestly ministry and of the holiness of this ministry." This obviously presupposes a genuine intimacy with Jesus, an imitation of Christ and a configuration to him.... The "mystery" of which the priest is the "steward" (cf. 1 Cor 4:1) is, ultimately, Jesus Christ Himself who, in the Spirit, is the Source of holiness and a call to sanctification. The "mystery" must be at the heart of the priest's daily life. It therefore requires great vigilance and a keen conscience. Again, the rite of ordination introduces the words cited above with the recommendation: "Understand, therefore, what you do." Saint Paul already warned the bishop Timothy: "Do not neglect the gift you have, which was given you by prophetic utterance when the elders [= presbyters] laid their hands upon you. Practice these duties" (1 Tim 4:14-15).[21]

---

[21] John Paul II, Retreat for priests and seminarians in Ars, October 6, 1986, no. 5.

If the priest does not seek this unity of life, he runs the risk of developing schizophrenia and living as a stranger to his own interior identity. What a tragedy! What a shipwreck! This danger of dissociating priestly life and private life is like a precipice that yawns at every moment beneath the feet of priests. They must tell themselves incessantly that they do not have on the one side their life as a priest, their "professional life," and on the other side their private life. To be a priest is not a profession; it is an identity that must become identification. At every moment, the priest must again realize that he must become existentially what he is essentially. Priestly holiness is at stake here. As early as the sixth century, Saint Gregory the Great knew this very well.

Priests who are not holy are not just mediocre. They drag toward evil those whom they are responsible for leading. The sin of a pastor is not a private affair. He wounds the whole flock with a deep wound. This shows how ambiguous and even incoherent the idea of a private life is for a priest. His whole life is priestly and pastoral because it is entirely consecrated to holiness, which is marked by his priestly anointing and commanded by his baptismal character and his priestly character. Holiness is not only desirable for a priest. It is a vital necessity for him and for the people of God.

Saint Gregory the Great, *Pastoral Rule*

Those who do not put into action in their lives the truths that they have learned in study must not assume pastoral responsibilities

There are some also who investigate spiritual precepts with cunning care, but what they penetrate with their understanding they trample on in their lives: all at once they teach the things which not by practice but by study they have learned; and what in words they preach by their manners they impugn. Whence it comes to pass that when the shepherd walks through steep places, the flock follows to the precipice. Hence it is that the Lord through the prophet complains of the contemptible knowledge of shepherds, saying, "When you yourselves had drunk most pure water, you fouled the residue with your feet; and My sheep fed on that which had been trodden by your feet, and drank that which your feet had fouled" (Ezek 34:18-19). For indeed the shepherds drink most pure water, when with a right understanding they imbibe the streams of truth. But to foul the same water with their feet is to corrupt the studies of holy meditation by evil living. And verily the sheep drink the water fouled by their feet, when any of those subject to them follow not the words which they hear, but only imitate the bad examples which they see. Thirsting for the things said, but perverted by the works observed, they take in mud with their draughts, as from polluted fountains.

Hence also it is written through the prophet, "A snare for the downfall of my people are evil priests" (Hos 5:1). Hence again the Lord through the prophet says of the priests, "They are made to be for a stumbling-block of iniquity to the house of Israel" (Ezek 44:12). For certainly no one does more harm in the Church than one who has the name and rank of sanctity, while he acts perversely. For him, when he transgresses, no one presumes to take to task; and the offense spreads forcibly for example, when out of reverence to his rank the sinner is honoured. But all who are unworthy would fly from the burden of so great guilt, if with the attentive ear of the heart they weighed the sentence of the Truth, "Whoever shall offend one of these little ones which believe *in me, it were better for him that a millstone were hanged about his neck, and he were drowned in the depth of the sea*" (Mt 18:6). By the millstone is expressed the round and labour of worldly life, and by the depth of the sea is denoted final damnation. Whosoever, then, having come to bear the outward show of sanctity, either by word or example destroys others, it had indeed been better for him that earthly deeds in open guise should press him down to death than that sacred offices should point him out to others as imitable in his wrong-doing; because, surely, if he fell alone, the pains of hell would torment him in more tolerable degree.[22]

The heavy burden of pastoral ministry; one must scorn adversity and fear prosperity

So much, then, have we briefly said, to show how great is the weight of government, lest whosoever is unequal to sacred offices of government should dare to profane them, and through lust of pre-eminence undertake a leadership of perdition. For hence it is that James affectionately deters us, saying, "Be not made many masters, my brethren" (Jas 3:1). Hence the Mediator between God and man Himself—He who, transcending the knowledge and understanding even of supernal spirits, reigns in heaven from eternity—on earth fled from receiving a kingdom.

---

[22] Gregory the Great, *Pastoral Rule*, I, 12, in *Nicene and Post-Nicene Fathers*, Second Series [NPNF 2], 12:2b–3a.

For it is written, "When Jesus therefore perceived that they would come and take Him by force, to make Him a king, He departed again into the mountain Himself alone" (Jn 6:15). For who could so blamelessly have had principality over men as He who would in fact have reigned over those whom He had Himself created? But, because He had come in the flesh to this end, that He might not only redeem us by His passion but also teach us by His conversation, offering Himself as an example to His followers, He would not be made a king; but He went of His own accord to the gibbet of the cross. He fled from the offered glory of pre-eminence, but desired the pain of an ignominious death; that so His members might learn to fly from the favours of the world, to be afraid of no terrors, to love adversity for the truth's sake, and to shrink in fear from prosperity; because this often defiles the heart through vain glory, while suffering purges it through sorrow.

In adversity the mind exalts itself, but in prosperity, even though it had once exalted itself, it brings itself low; in success man forgets himself, but in trials, even perforce and against his will, he is recalled to memory of what he is; when all goes well, even good things done aforetime often come to nothing, but in suffering, faults even of long standing are wiped away. For commonly in the school of adversity the heart is subdued under discipline, while, on sudden attainment of great authority, it is immediately changed and becomes elated through familiarity with glory.[23]

---

[23] *Pastoral Rule*, I, 3, p. 3ab.

*The pastor should have compassion
on each of his sheep individually and
should surpass all the faithful in contemplation*

The ruler should be a near neighbour to every one in
sympathy, and exalted above all in contemplation, so that
through the bowels of loving-kindness he may transfer the
infirmities of others to himself, and by loftiness of specu-
lation transcend even himself in his aspiration after the
invisible; lest either in seeking high things he despise the
weak things of his neighbours, or in suiting himself to the
weak things of his neighbours he relinquish his aspiration
after high things.... [Saint Paul,] being joined at once to the
things of heaven and to the things of earth by the bond of
charity, though in himself mightily caught up in the power
of the Spirit into the heights above, yet among others, in
his loving-kindness, he is content to become weak. Hence,
therefore, he says, "Who is weak, and I am not weak? Who
is offended, and I burn not?" (2 Cor 11:29). Hence again
he says, "Unto the Jews I became as a Jew" (1 Cor 9:20).
Now he exhibited this behaviour not by losing hold of his
faith, but by extending his loving-kindness; so as, by transferring in a figure the person of unbelievers to himself, to
learn from himself how they ought to have compassion
shown them; to the end that he might bestow on them
what he would have rightly wished to have had bestowed
upon himself, had he been as they. Hence again he says,
"Whether we be beside ourselves, it is to God: or whether
we be sober, it is for you" (2 Cor 5:13). For he had known
how both to transcend himself in contemplation, and to
accommodate himself to his hearers in condescension....

He who is wrapped into contemplation within [the sanctuary] is busied outside with the affairs of those who are subject to infirmity. Within he considers the secret things of God; without he carries the burdens of the carnal. And also concerning doubtful matters [Moses] always recurs to the tabernacle, to consult the Lord before the Ark of the Covenant; affording without doubt an example to rulers; that, when in the outside world they are uncertain how to order things, they should return to their own soul as though to the tabernacle, and, as before the Ark of the Covenant, consult the Lord, if so, they may search within themselves the pages of sacred utterance concerning that whereof they doubt.[24]

Meditation

Pope Saint Gregory gives us, then, a remedy for priestly hypocrisy, the attitude of acting in a way that contradicts one's being. He proposes three methods. The first is to scorn adversity and to fear prosperity. I would translate this: to refuse to conform our judgment to the world's criteria. Since the priest is shielded from worldly ties and devoted completely to God, he must resolutely leave the world while remaining in the world. This is what Saint John exhorts us to do in his first letter, when he says, "I write to you, young men, because you are strong, and the word of God abides in you, and you have overcome the Evil One. Do not love the world or the things in the world. If any one loves the world, love for the Father is not in him" (1 Jn 2:14–15).

[24] *Pastoral Rule*, II, 5, p. 12b–13b.

The world that we, young priests and older ones, must not love and to which we must not be conformed is not, as we know very well, the world that God created and loves. Nor is it the persons of the world to whom, on the contrary, we must always go—above all, the poor and the poorest of the poor—to proclaim to them the gospel of Jesus Christ, to love them and serve them humbly and generously. No! The world that should not be loved is another world; it is the world as it has become under the dominion of Satan and sin, the world of ideologies that are directly opposed to God, deny human nature and its laws, destroy human lives and mutilate them, and demolish moral principles, the family, and societies. It is what we call adapting to the spirit of the times, conformism, consensus. A great British poet of the last century, T. S. Eliot, wrote three verses that say more about this than entire books:

> In a world of fugitives,
> the person taking the opposite direction
> will appear to run away.[25]

Dear young priests, and you older members of the priesthood, allow me to tell you again with Saint John: "You have overcome the Evil One!" Be one of those who take the opposite direction. Dare to go against the current of our decadent societies. For us Christians, the opposite direction is not a place. It is a Person: it is Jesus Christ, Our Lord, our God, and our Redeemer—the one and only Redeemer of the world. Follow Him; He is the one way that leads you to the Father and the full realization of your priesthood. This demands that you agree to carry the Cross and that you calmly come to terms with failure and the world's scorn. This demands that you reject all worldly success and all media popularity.

[25] T. S. Eliot, *The Family Reunion.*

For worldly people, success and media popularity are the proof of success. For the priest, trials and the Cross are the guarantee that you are on the right path: Christ's. Worldly success shuts the soul away in secular glory. The hearts becomes bogged down in it. It becomes a prisoner. It loses all its prophetic courage. One fears being critiqued in the media. Then, in order to be well regarded by them and to be at ease, one adopts their language, one submits to their ideologies. One starts to censor or to dilute the Word of God with the excuse that if we handed it on as it came from the mouth of God, it would not be fitting or would not be accepted. One lives in fear of being treated as fanatics, intransigents, hard-liners, with the risk of being detested and rejected. The priest then becomes a "communicant" at the service of an ideology. We know, however, that we are here not just to be loved but in order to love. We are here not to be approved but in order to proclaim the truth. We are here not to be popular but to serve. If we want approval, if we seek to be popular, we will drift until we no longer see clearly and are no longer able say what it is our duty to say. In season and out of season, we must proclaim the truth that Jesus and His gospel are, whether it pleases people or provokes rejection and brings down on us hatred, persecution, and martyrdom. This is the recommendation that God makes to us when he tells us: "Son of man, I send you to the sons of Israel, to a nation of rebels, who have rebelled against me; they and their fathers have transgressed against me to this very day.... I send you to them; and you shall say to them, 'Thus says the Lord God'" (Ezek 2:3-4). Truth is bothersome—this is nothing new. Witnesses to the truth have always annoyed the proud, the clever, or the skeptics. This is why, in former times, they did away with Socrates, the prophets of Israel, the Precursor John the Baptist, and Jesus the Savior Himself, making Him suffer the most horrible torture, the agony of the Cross. The Kingdom of God will come not through the cheering of the people but rather through the welcome that we give to our Heavenly Father.

The ministry and teaching of Jesus testify that He had been sent by the Father. If we open our lives to Him, we pass from knowledge about what He said and did to a reception of the Faith and sincere adherence to His Word of Life. Nowadays when, on the social networks, we incessantly count the number of persons who follow our pages or like our posts, there is a great danger of seeking success more than the Cross.

On Good Friday, Jesus was very unpopular. Everyone was shouting, "This man deserves death. Crucify Him, crucify Him!" They crucified Him at the place called Golgotha. At Golgotha, He was fully a priest. Jesus, the Supreme Priest, reaches the height of His priesthood covered with spittle, humiliation, and insults; His face swollen; alone, abandoned on the Cross, and not amid the hosannas of Palm Sunday. Let us remember this when we judge our lives as priests! Let us remember, Saint Gregory insists, that Jesus "fled from the offered glory of pre-eminence, but desired the pain of an ignominious death; that so His members might learn to fly from the favours of the world, to be afraid of no terrors, to love adversity for the truth's sake, and to shrink in fear from prosperity; because this often defiles the heart through vain glory, while suffering purges it through sorrow."

The second important method that Saint Gregory gives us is to open our hearts to compassion: "In his loving-kindness, he is content to become weak. Hence, therefore, [Saint Paul] says, 'Who is weak, and I am not weak? Who is offended, and I burn not?' (2 Cor 11:29)." The Letter to the Hebrews states that we have a High Priest, Christ, who is able to have compassion on our miseries. "For every high priest chosen from among men is appointed to act on behalf of men in relation to God, to offer gifts and sacrifices for sins. He can deal gently with the ignorant and wayward, since he himself is beset with weakness" (Heb 5:1–2). To make Christ present is to make present this heart that is capable of being open to the suffering of others. The heart of the priest must suffer with those who suffer. He must take on this suffering, weep with those who weep.

We know very well that the priest is the one whom people come to see when they have exhausted all other possibilities. Everyone should be sure of always finding in him a listening heart, a man who is never indifferent. Sometimes a priest is not in a position to give alms or to find a solution to the problems that someone confides to him. But he can always listen, be compassionate, love, and pray. He is the universal, benevolent friend.

Making our hearts "kindly" and "weak," as Saint Gregory says, is in no way a compromise or a diminution of the truth. Pope Saint Gregory the Great explains this: the priest must act "not by losing hold of his faith, but by extending his loving-kindness; so as, by transferring in a figure the person of unbelievers to himself, to learn from himself how they ought to have compassion shown them." Indeed, this is a question of experience. Every priest must take on the suffering of desperate unbelievers, of humiliated fathers of families, of exhausted mothers, of disoriented children. To listen to them with an open heart is to have an experience of their own suffering.

"Why do this?" you will ask me. In order to offer this suffering to the Father of mercies, in order to pray, to offer on the paten at the Offertory the suffering of the world, so that it might ascend to the heart of the Trinity where the only true happiness resides. The priest has this duty to accept suffering so as to make it ascend to the heart of the Father and to transmit the love of God to the hearts of the poor. He is a mediator of suffering and of love.

This presupposes a third antidote to hypocrisy: the incessant back-and-forth from prayer to action. This is not just a matter of keeping set times for prayer. That is necessary but not sufficient. Even in the midst of each action, each encounter, it is a matter of entering regularly into the innermost depth of the heart, where God dwells. As Saint Gregory again says:

> In the tabernacle ... [the priest] considers the secret things of God; outside he carries the burdens of human affairs. And also concerning doubtful matters [Moses] always recurs to the tabernacle, to consult the Lord before the Ark of the Covenant; affording without doubt an example to rulers [of the Churches]; that, when in the outside world they are uncertain how to order things, they should return to their own soul as though to the tabernacle, and, as before the Ark of the Covenant, consult the Lord, if so, they may search within themselves the pages of sacred utterance concerning that whereof they doubt.

Thus, once a decision has been made in the Lord's presence and with Him, the action, too, must become incessant prayer. Even when the priest is listening, consoling, or blessing, an altogether interior prayer ascends to God to the rhythm of his heartbeat.

III

The Priest: Nothing and Everything

Based on a meditation by Saint John Chrysostom

———— ◁∞▷ ————

Introduction

The following saying is attributed to Saint Norbert: "O priest, who are you? You are not from yourself, since you are nothing. You are not for yourself, since you are the spouse of the Church. You are not your own, since you are the servant of all. You are not yourself, since you are God. Who are you, then? Nothing and everything." These words correctly state the mystery of the priesthood. We ask a priest to be acquainted with the poor and the rich, the sick and the powerful; to be close to persons belonging to the nobility and to persons of humble social origin. We require that he be able to guide, teach, and sanctify. We expect him to counsel spouses and business leaders, to be full of compassion for those who suffer, to climb the steps to the altar every day to renew the sacrifice of Calvary. We expect the priest to know "how one ought to behave in the household of God, which is the Church of the living God, the pillar and bulwark of the truth" (1 Tim 3:15). The priest must not conceal the truth for anything in the world. Like Jesus, he must be able to say: "For this I was born, and for this I have come into the world, to bear witness to the truth. Every one who is of the truth hears my voice" (Jn 18:37). In the name of peace and social harmony, many people today ask the Church to conceal the truths of the Christian faith when She intervenes publicly. Similarly, this peace is utilized to justify the culpable inaction and silence of pastors with regard to those who endanger the very unity of the Church and distort Her teaching. In the Encyclical Letter *Caritas in veritate* by Benedict XVI, we read:

> Charity in truth (*caritas in veritate*), to which Jesus Christ bore witness by his earthly life and especially by his death and resurrection, is the principal driving force behind the authentic development of every person and of all humanity....
>
> Hence the need to link charity with truth not only in the sequence, pointed out by Saint Paul, of *veritas in caritate* (Eph 4:15), but also in the inverse and complementary sequence of *caritas in veritate*. Truth needs to be sought, found and expressed within the "economy" of charity, but charity in its turn needs to be understood, confirmed and practised in the light of truth.[26]

Truth comes before everything else. For if peace is a result of charity and love, can there be any authentic peace where the truth is denied? It seems to me that we ought to adopt without hesitation what Blaise Pascal writes:

> As peace in States has for its sole object the safe preservation of the property of the people, so the peace of the

---

[26] Benedict XVI, *Caritas in veritate* (July 7, 2009), nos. 1 and 2.

Church has for its sole object the safe preservation of truth, her property and the treasure where her heart is. And [just] as to allow the enemy to enter into a State, and pillage without opposition, for fear of troubling repose, would be to work against the good of peace, because peace, being only just and useful for the security of property, becomes unjust and harmful when it suffers property to be destroyed, while war in the defence of property becomes just and necessary ... [so too] in the Church, when truth is assailed by the enemies of faith, when men would tear it from the heart of the faithful, and cause error to reign there, to remain in peace is rather to betray than to serve the Church, to ruin rather than defend. And as it is plainly a crime to trouble peace where truth reigns, so is it also a crime to rest in peace when truth is destroyed. There is then a time when peace is just, and another when it is unjust. And it is written that "there is a time for peace and a time for war," and it is the interest of truth to discern them. But there is not a time for truth and a time for error, and it is written, on the contrary, that "the truth of God abideth for ever"; and this is why Jesus Christ, who said that he came to bring peace, said also that he came to bring war. But he did not say that he came to bring both truth and falsehood. Truth is then the first rule and the ultimate end of things.[27]

Yes, we expect a priest to be a peacemaker, a man of God, and therefore a witness to the truth.

---

[27] *The Thoughts of Blaise Pascal*, translated from the text of M. Auguste Molinier by C. Kegan Paul (London: George Bell and Sons, 1901), 281.

———— ⟨∞⟩ ————

Saint John Chrysostom,
Dialogue on the Priesthood

Priests are the salt of the earth. But who would easily put up with my lack of understanding, and my inexperience in all things, but thou, who hast been wont to love me beyond measure[?] For the priest ought not only to be thus pure a one who has been dignified with so high a ministry, but very discreet, and skilled in many matters, and to be as well versed in the affairs of this life as they who are engaged in the world, and yet to be free from them all more than the recluses who occupy the mountains. For since he must mix with men who have wives, and who bring up children, who possess servants, and are surrounded with wealth, and fill public positions, and are persons of influence, he too should be a many-sided man—I say many-sided, not unreal, nor yet fawning and hypocritical, but full of much freedom and assurance, and knowing how to adapt himself profitably, where the circumstances of the case require it, and to be both kind and severe, for it is not possible to treat all those under one's authority on one plan, since neither is it well for physicians to apply one course of treatment to all their sick, nor for a pilot to know but one way of contending with the winds. For, indeed, continual storms beset this ship of ours, and these storms do not assail from without only, but take their rise from within, and there is need of much condescension, and circumspection, and all these different matters have one end in view, the glory of God, and the edifying of the Church....

But if any inquire about his relations with God, he will find the others to be as nothing, since these require a greater and more thorough earnestness. For he who acts as an ambassador on behalf of the whole city—but why do I say the city? On behalf of the whole world indeed—prays that God would be merciful to the sins of all, not only of the living, but also of the departed. What manner of man ought he to be? For my part I think that the boldness of speech of Moses and Elias, is insufficient for such supplication. For as though he were entrusted with the whole world and were himself the father of all men, he draws near to God, beseeching that wars may be extinguished everywhere, that tumults may be quelled; asking for peace and plenty, and a swift deliverance from all the ills that beset each one, publicly and privately; and he ought as much to excel in every respect all those on whose behalf he prays, as rulers should excel their subjects. And whenever he invokes the Holy Spirit, and offers the most dread sacrifice, and constantly handles the common Lord of all, tell me what rank shall we give him? What great purity and what real piety must we demand of him? For consider what manner of hands they ought to be which minister in these things, and of what kind his tongue which utters such words, and ought not the soul which receives so great a Spirit to be purer and holier than anything in the world? At such a time angels stand by the priest; and the whole sanctuary, and the space round about the altar, is filled with the powers of heaven, in honor of Him who lieth thereon. For this, indeed, is capable of being proved from the very rites which are being then celebrated. . . .

And dost thou not yet tremble to introduce a soul into so sacred a mystery of this priesthood, one robed in filthy raiment, whom Christ has shut out from the rest of the band of guests? The soul of the priest should shine like a light beaming over the whole world. But mine has so great darkness overhanging it, because of my evil conscience, as to be always cast down and never able to look up with confidence to its Lord.[28]

Meditation

Who would dare to say, "I am ready for all that"? Who could ever say, "I am up to it"? "How frightening it is to be a priest!... A priest is a man who takes God's place, a man who is vested with all the power of God," the Curé of Ars used to say.[29] Fear is certainly something necessary for a priest. Not servile fear, being afraid of God, the fear of what others may think: this immature feeling makes someone a slave. It shows a secret pride, as if we refused to let truth reveal our true weakness. The fear necessary for a priest is filial, joyous fear—the kind that is based on calm realism about our limits and makes us tremble with amazement and gratitude at the gift that God gives. A priest must marvel every day: "Christ wants to continue His work today through me, although I am poor, unworthy, and so inadequate." Unless we tremble in gratitude and adoration before the greatness of the gift, we run the risk of claiming our vocation as our own. Nothing could be worse. It would open the door to all sorts of abuses. But in order

---

[28] John Chrysostom, *On the Priesthood* VI, 4–5, *Nicene and Post-Nicene Fathers*, First Series [NPNF 1] 9:76a–77a], emended.

[29] Bernard Nodet, *Jean-Marie Vianney, curé d'Ars: Sa pensée, son coeur* (Paris: Éditions du Cerf, 2006), 99.

to remain in this salutary fear, it is advisable to consider unceasingly the greatness of the gift. Trivializing the priesthood would be a wrong turn. Trying to make the priest a man like all the others would be a colossal error. In many countries, Christians have the custom of kissing the priest's hands on the day of his ordination. Why venerate his hands? What priest would be foolish enough to think that his personality was being venerated in this way? In this gesture, inspired by the intuition of the people of God, their *sensus fidei*, Christ is the one being venerated, not the priest, and through his hands, which have just been anointed with the Holy Chrism, they honor the pierced hands of Christ crucified.

Bishops know this very well. During the liturgy, there are multiple signs of veneration and respect for them. Is it because they are saints or princes of the Church? Not at all. These gestures are addressed to the Good Shepherd, Who presides at the liturgy in them. This is why, when they preside at the liturgy in Christ's name, they must comport themselves in a manner that is noble, dignified, grand, humble, and little at the same time. They must be self-effacing in the presence of the High Priest Jesus Christ, so that He is the one who appears, and not they. It is not a sign of progress or a mark of simplicity for a bishop or a priest to fall into the crude trap of banality, mediocrity, superficiality, or disgusting vulgarity. This is perhaps the reason why it is good for the priest to disappear beneath the liturgical vestments, for the chasuble and the alb to cover his body entirely: so that everyone knows very well that we do not expect a priest to impose his unique, brilliant personality but, rather, to let Jesus Christ appear through him.

Does this mean that he should have no personality and end up denying his humanity? On the contrary, he must make it grow, accept it in a balanced way so as to conform it deeply to the Heart of Christ. We do not ask the priest to be insipid but, rather, to let

Christ take possession of his gifts, personality, and temperament. In order for a violin to be a good instrument in the artist's hands, it has to be tuned correctly. Similarly, a priest must work for the orderly and balanced flourishing of his human and moral virtues so as to be a good instrument in the hands of the Divine Artist.

Therefore, he must not be afraid of his human personality or of the talents that the Creator has engraved on it. Similarly, he must work incessantly on his competence in theology, exegesis, moral theology, spirituality, canon law, and Church history. He must work, because being an instrument never means neglecting to do our own part. It seems to me that every month priests ought to gather around the One who is the Way, the Truth, and the Life—Jesus Christ—to discuss together a point of moral or pastoral theology. Every year they should give themselves a few days to study a point of theology in greater depth or to read some Magisterial teaching. Without this work, one runs the risk of becoming less flexible in God's hands. Without this work, how could one's homilies be nourishing for the faithful? We ask the Holy Spirit for His light, but unless we labor, we force Him to work miracles for us. The faithful have the right to be demanding. They have the right and the duty to rebuke fraternally a priest who is not exactly faithful to the teaching of the Church. Christians have a right to healthy, substantial, rich food so that their spiritual and human life might flourish.

The more a priest works and is formed, the more he will realize that he is not the master of his knowledge and competence but an unworthy agent entrusted with the revelation of the Most High God. The more deeply assured he is of this, the more overjoyed he will be at the beauty of his vocation.

IV

Priest, Who Are You?

Based on a meditation by Saint John Paul II

Introduction

Above all, we must understand who the priest is. We no longer know this. Many priests are hesitant about their identity. Many of the faithful expect from their priest something other than what he is. Here it is not a question of launching into a major theological treatise. Who could answer our question? Would we have to turn to a specialist, a professional theologian, a professor? But then how could we avoid being prisoners of a school of thought, an opinion, a fashion, or the ideological and political trends of the moment? According to a German manuscript:

A priest must be simultaneously great and small, noble-minded as though of royal blood, simple and natural as though of peasant stock; a hero at self-conquest, a man who has fought along with God; a source of sanctification, a sinner whom God has forgiven. The master of his desires, a servant for the timid and the weak, who does not bow to the mighty, but rather bends down to the poor. A disciple of his Lord, the leader of his flock. A beggar with wide-open hands, a bringer of countless gifts; a man on the battlefield, a mother to comfort the sick. With the wisdom of age and the trust of a child, straining toward the heights with his feet on the ground; made for joy, familiar with suffering, far from all desire; clear-sighted, speaking frankly; a friend of peace, an enemy of inertia, constant forever, so different from me!

The priesthood cannot be constantly redefined to suit the current mood or to respond to regional or cultural pastoral needs. Who, then, can tell us who a priest is for God? Only the Church can do that. She has always taught, clarified, and defined. She tells Her priests who they are. She tells the people of God who their pastors are. This long, unbroken chain of teaching, texts, and homilies starts with Jesus and ends at today's Magisterium. Through this chain, we take the hand of Christ Himself. This uninterrupted transmission has a name: living Tradition. The Church transmits the teaching of Jesus while clarifying it and exploring it in greater depth. Through the life of Christians, She understands more and more profoundly what She must hand down. This is why this Tradition is living: it grows and is renewed unceasingly so as to give us more and more light about what the Church has received as a deposit, which does not change and never will change.

What does Tradition tell us about the priest? The latest major insight that the Church gave us was Vatican Council II. In it She elaborated in greater depth Her teaching about the priestly identity. She intended to take a contemplative and spiritual look at the whole people of God. In *Lumen gentium*, She brought to light the profound and necessary complementary relation between the states of life of baptized persons: the state of life of laypeople, the state of life of priests, and the state of life of religious. Saint Paul VI had asked for a deeper examination of the particular identity of each of these three states of life so as to assimilate more profoundly the teaching of Vatican Council II. This was the object of three synods, which gave rise to three Apostolic Exhortations by Saint John Paul II: *Christifideles laici*, on the vocation and the mission of the lay faithful in the Church and in the world (December 30, 1988); *Pastores dabo vobis*, on the formation of priests in the circumstances of the present day (March 25, 1992); *Vita consecrata*, on the consecrated life and its mission in the Church and in the world (March 25, 1996). This reflection was completed by the publication of a document on the mystery and the ministry of the bishop, *Pastores gregis* (October 16, 2003).

It seems to me that the Council's main insight was to emphasize that the three states of life are rooted in Baptism. They are therefore three modes, three specific manners of living out the baptismal dynamism—in other words, the vocation to holiness.

In former times, in the Old Covenant, only the priests owned sacred garments that they were supposed to put on for the ceremonies (Ex 28:4-43; Joel 2:28-30). Saint Paul assures us that this privilege is now a thing of the past (Acts 2:17-18; 21:9; 2 Cor 1:21). He writes to the Galatians: "For as many of you as were baptized into Christ have put on Christ" (Gal 3:27). Moreover, all baptized persons have received the anointing that was formerly reserved to the high priest alone. He alone was allowed, once a year, to enter into the Holy of Holies; today, faith in Jesus Christ gives to us all free access to it through His blood:

> Therefore, brethren, since we have confidence to enter the sanctuary by the blood of Jesus, by the new and living way which he opened for us through the curtain, that is,

through his flesh, and since we have a great priest over the
house of God, let us draw near with a true heart in full
assurance of faith, with our hearts sprinkled clean from
an evil conscience and our bodies washed with pure water.
(Heb 10:19–22)

Whereas only Aaron's descendants touched the holy oblations,
the one priestly body of the Church is fed on the one Eucharistic
Bread. But if all the baptized faithful have put on Christ, what is
the specific character of the ministerial priest?

Perhaps in the past, the priesthood could be reduced to the
ability to perform acts to serve the life of Christians. It was possible
to forget that the priestly life is a specific path of holiness rooted
in Baptism. To underscore the capital importance of the sacraments in the life of the Church, the priesthood was sometimes
reduced to the power to consecrate the Eucharist and to absolve
sins. Of course, these acts are central in the life of a priest. Of
course, this power (in the Latin sense of *potestas*) is real. But if this
is overemphasized, there is a danger of reducing the priesthood
to a function, to "doing something." Now, the priest is valuable
in the first place for what he is and not for what he does. Far be
it from us, then, to think of denying or even just relativizing this
specifically priestly power of consecrating and absolving. But we
cannot reduce the priest to being an "administrator of sacraments."

What is he, then, deep down? What is his being? His essence,
his definition? I think that the Council gives us a very profound
answer that theology has not yet reflected on in sufficient depth. It
invites us to consider the unity of the Sacrament of Holy Orders
(deacons, priests, and bishops) in terms of the episcopal order.
Indeed, *Lumen gentium* states very clearly that in the episcopate is
found "the fullness of the priesthood," the "acme [total reality] of

the sacred ministry" (*sacri ministerii summa*). Therefore, we must look to the sacramental reality of the episcopate in order to understand the essence of the Sacrament of Holy Orders, to understand what priests are. Now, the definition of the episcopate that the Council gives us is quite clear: by virtue of the sacred character imprinted on their souls by the sacrament:

> Bishops, in a resplendent and visible manner, take the place of Christ himself, teacher, shepherd, and priest, and act as his representatives (*in eius persona*, in his Person).... In the person of the bishops, then, to whom the priests render assistance, the Lord Jesus Christ, supreme high priest, is present in the midst of the faithful.[30]

How I wish that the whole Church understood this major, definitive teaching of the Council! Here we have the definition of the priest; here is his essence, his profound identity! He is the one who takes the place of Christ Himself and acts in His person. I have often written that the priest is not only an *alter Christus* [another Christ] but *ipse Christus* [Christ Himself]. Some people have reproached me vehemently for doing so. In the vocabulary of the Fathers of the Church, the expression *alter Christus* applies to every baptized Christian, but it can be used *a fortiori*, "all the more," with regard to the priest, according to Saint John Paul II and Benedict XVI. Saint Josemaría Escrivá goes further, stating that every Christian, by his Baptism, is *ipse Christus*. I would like to clarify matters here on the basis of the Council.

The priest is not another Christ alongside Christ. He is Christ Himself, Who continues Himself sacramentally. The directory

---

[30] Vatican Council II, Dogmatic Constitution on the Church *Lumen gentium* (November 21, 1964), no. 21.

Apostolorum successores (§12), published in 2004, teaches us that, being ontologically configured to Christ, the priest becomes a "sacrament of Christ himself," present and active in his ministry. As the Council says, the priest takes the place of Christ and acts in His person (*in persona*). When we say that the priest is *ipse Christus*, obviously this does not mean that he is "the Word who was with the Father" (cf. Jn 1:1) or that he would be like a new incarnation. That would be plainly false and would open the door to all sorts of abuses. It does not mean, either, that the priest, by his ordination, suddenly became a saint as if by magic. We know very well that not all priests are saints! I know it firsthand, and my confessor even more so, since he knows all my miseries and how often I grow weary in aiming for holiness.

This identification is not on the psychological level. We know that pedophile priests have sometimes deeply perverted this notion. They made their victims believe that everything that they demanded was willed by Christ since they were priests. On the contrary, far from creating a kind of psychological impunity, this identification with Christ ought to be a source of constant demands on the priest. He should ceaselessly ask himself: Is my life in conformity with Christ's? Am I, like Him, the servant of all?

The Council clearly explains that the root of this priestly being is the sacred character imprinted by the sacrament. This character shapes our souls. It gives our souls their identity. It establishes the priestly state of life—in other words, a priest's specific way of living out his baptismal holiness. For a priest, this will be a matter of taking the place of Christ and of acting not only in His Name but in His Person. To be a priest is to make Christ present. This guarantees neither my holiness nor my competence! Yet it is my being, my profound and definitive identity in the Church. The priest makes present Christ, the Priest, Shepherd, and Bridegroom of the Church.

When the priest visits a sick person, he makes present to this suffering member of the Church the Person of Christ the Priest. It may be that during this visit, he is clumsy and less humanly competent than a nun or a layman who is better trained in this work of charity. But there is one thing that he alone can do: instrumentally make Christ, the Priest and Shepherd, present to this sick person. This presence culminates in the sacramental acts: giving the Body of Christ, absolving sins, anointing with the holy oil of the sick. This presence is an instrumental way of being. Christ, the Priest and Shepherd, is willing to have need of the priest's humanity, which is identified with His own through the sacramental character, in order to make Himself present. The whole person of the priest becomes an instrument of Christ. He represents Christ not as an ambassador represents a head of state but by "re-presenting" Him, by making Him present through his own person, which becomes a prolongation of Christ's humanity. This is why the secret of the confessional is absolute. What the priest hears belongs to Christ alone. A priest who tells others the sins that he hears in the confessional commits a very grave sin; he insults God and the penitents. In doing that, he betrays Christ and does not identify with Christ, and therefore, his bishop ought to withdraw from him permanently his faculty to hear confessions.

Cardinal Jean-Marie Lustiger liked to remind priests: "We have to be so bold as to say: We are Christ! That is the identity of the priest: the identity of Christ."[31]

Dear Christians, what a wonder! The priest is not an intermediary, a screen between Christ and us. On the contrary, through him, through his person marked by the sacramental character, Jesus

[31] Cardinal Jean-Marie Lustiger, Homily at the ordination of priests, June 28, 1986.

Himself touches me, blesses me, looks at me, and speaks to me! I am in contact with the humanity of Jesus. When a priest teaches the catechism to children, he may be clumsy. Very often, laypersons, men or women, are more gifted and better prepared for that delicate art of proclaiming God to children. But when a poor priest speaks to children, truly, mysteriously, sacramentally, Jesus, the Good Shepherd, is present in their midst. This presence is not substantial, like the Eucharistic presence, but it is sacramental, as Saint John Paul II teaches explicitly—in other words, it is simultaneously a sign and a reality. The Council, moreover, recalls this presence of Christ in the priest when it states that "Christ is always present in his Church, especially in her liturgical celebrations. He is present in the Sacrifice of the Mass not only in the person of his minister, 'the same now offering, through the ministry of priests, who formerly offered himself on the cross,' but especially in the eucharistic species."[32]

Moreover, it is important to emphasize that this presence is ministerial. The priest's soul is the soul of a minister—in other words, of a servant. This is why no one can be a priest without being a deacon. In order to make present Christ the Shepherd and *a fortiori* Christ the Head, it is necessary first to make present Christ the Servant. This ministerial presence of Christ, which defines priestly identity, by no means implies any automatic sanctity of the priest. We will return to this later. This is a great mystery. Sometimes Jesus makes Himself present through the ministry of unworthy priests. But we know now that priestly holiness will be this combat, this struggle to live out concretely, at every moment, the fullness of this ministerial being: being the instrument through which Jesus the Shepherd makes Himself present to His Church.

---

[32] Vatican Council II, Constitution on the Sacred Liturgy *Sacrosanctum Concilium* (December 4, 1963), no. 7.

Saint John Paul II, *Pastores dabo vobis*

For the sake of this universal priesthood of the new covenant Jesus gathered disciples during his earthly mission (cf. Lk 10:1-12), and with a specific and authoritative mandate he called and appointed the Twelve "to be with him, and to be sent out to preach and have authority to cast out demons" (Mk 3:14-15).

For this reason, already during his public ministry (cf. Mt 16:18), and then most fully after his death and resurrection (cf. Mt 28:16-20; Jn 20; 21), Jesus had conferred on Peter and the Twelve entirely special powers with regard to the future community and the evangelization of all peoples. After having called them to follow him, he kept them at his side and lived with them, imparting his teaching of salvation to them through word and example, and finally he sent them out to all mankind. To enable them to carry out this mission Jesus confers upon the apostles, by a specific paschal outpouring of the Holy Spirit, the same messianic authority which he had received from the Father, conferred in its fullness in his resurrection: "All authority in heaven and on earth has been given to me. Go therefore and make disciples of all nations, baptizing them in the name of the Father and of the Son and of the Holy Spirit, teaching them to observe all that I have commanded you; and lo, I am with you always, to the close of the age" (Mt 28:18-20).

Jesus thus established a close relationship between the ministry entrusted to the apostles and his own mission: "He who receives you receives me, and he who receives me receives him who sent me" (Mt 10:40); "He who hears you hears me, and he who rejects you rejects me, and he who rejects me rejects him who sent me" (Lk 10:16). Indeed, in the light of the paschal event of the death and resurrection, the fourth Gospel affirms this with great force and clarity: "As the Father has sent me, even so I send you" (Jn 20:21; cf. 13:20; 17:18). Just as Jesus has a mission which comes to him directly from God and makes present the very authority of God (cf. Mt 7:29; 21:23; Mk 1:27; 11:28; Lk 20:2; 24:19), so too the apostles have a mission which comes to them from Jesus. And just as "the Son can do nothing of his own accord" (Jn 5:19) such that his teaching is not his own but the teaching of the One who sent him (cf. Jn 7:16), so Jesus says to the apostles: "Apart from me you can do nothing" (Jn 15:5). Their mission is not theirs but is the same mission of Jesus. All this is possible not as a result of human abilities, but only with the "gift" of Christ and his Spirit, with the "sacrament": "Receive the Holy Spirit. If you forgive the sins of any, they are forgiven; if you retain the sins of any, they are retained" (Jn 20:22-23). And so the apostles, not by any special merit of their own, but only through a gratuitous participation in the grace of Christ, prolong throughout history to the end of time the same mission of Jesus on behalf of humanity.

The sign and presupposition of the authenticity and fruitfulness of this mission is the apostles' unity with Jesus and, in him, with one another and with the Father—as the priestly prayer of our Lord, which sums up his mission, bears witness (cf. Jn 17:20-23).

In their turn, the apostles, appointed by the Lord, progressively carried out their mission by calling—in various but complementary ways—other men as bishops, as priests and as deacons in order to fulfill the command of the risen Jesus who sent them forth to all people in every age.

The writings of the New Testament are unanimous in stressing that it is the same Spirit of Christ who introduces these men chosen from among their brethren into the ministry. Through the laying on of hands (cf. Acts 6:6; 1 Tim 4:14; 5:22; 2 Tim 1:6), which transmits the gift of the Spirit, they are called and empowered to continue the same ministry of reconciliation, of shepherding the flock of God and of teaching (cf. Acts 20:28; 1 Pet 5:2).

Therefore, priests are called to prolong the presence of Christ, the one high priest, embodying his way of life and making him visible in the midst of the flock entrusted to their care. We find this clearly and precisely stated in the First Letter of Peter: "I exhort the elders among you, as a fellow elder and a witness of the sufferings of Christ as well as a partaker in the glory that is to be revealed. Tend the flock of God that is your charge, not by constraint but willingly, not for shameful gain but eagerly, not as domineering over those in your charge but being examples to the flock. And when the chief Shepherd is manifested you will obtain the unfading crown of glory" (1 Pet 5:1-4).

In the Church and on behalf of the Church, priests are a sacramental representation of Jesus Christ—the head and shepherd[33]—authoritatively proclaiming his word, repeating his acts of forgiveness and his offer of salvation—particularly in Baptism, Penance and the Eucharist, showing his loving concern to the point of a total gift of self for the flock, which

[33] Emphasis ours.

they gather into unity and lead to the Father through Christ and in the Spirit. In a word, priests exist and act in order to proclaim the Gospel to the world and to build up the Church in the name and person of Christ the Head and Shepherd.

This is the ordinary and proper way in which ordained ministers share in the one priesthood of Christ. By the sacramental anointing of Holy Orders, the Holy Spirit configures them in a new and special way to Jesus Christ the Head and Shepherd; he forms and strengthens them with his pastoral charity; and he gives them an authoritative role in the Church as servants of the proclamation of the Gospel to every people and of the fullness of Christian life of all the baptized.

The truth of the priest as it emerges from the Word of God, that is, from Jesus Christ himself and from his constitutive plan for the Church, is thus proclaimed with joyful gratitude by the Preface of the liturgy of the Chrism Mass: "For by the anointing of the Holy Spirit you made your Only Begotten Son High Priest of the new and eternal covenant, and by your wondrous design were pleased to decree that his one Priesthood should continue in the Church. Christ ... with a brother's kindness ... also chooses men to become sharers in his sacred ministry through the laying on of hands. ... They give up their lives for you and for the salvation of their brothers and sisters ... and offer you a constant witness of faith and love."

The priest's fundamental relationship is to Jesus Christ, Head and Shepherd. Indeed, the priest participates in a specific and authoritative way in the "consecration/anointing" and in the "mission" of Christ (cf. Lk 4:18-19). But intimately linked to this relationship is the priest's relationship with the Church. It is not a question of "relations" which are merely juxtaposed, but rather of ones which are interiorly united in a kind of mutual immanence. The priest's relation to the Church is inscribed in the very relation which the priest has to Christ, such that the "sacramental representation" to Christ serves as the basis and inspiration for the relation of the priest to the Church.

In this sense the Synod Fathers wrote: "

> *Inasmuch as he represents Christ the Head, Shepherd and Spouse of the Church, the priest is placed not only in the Church but also in the forefront of the Church.*[34]
> The priesthood, along with the word of God and the sacramental signs which it serves, belongs to the constitutive elements of the Church. The ministry of the priest is entirely on behalf of the Church; it aims at promoting the exercise of the common priesthood of the entire People of God; it is ordered not only to the particular Church but also to the universal Church (*Presbyterorum Ordinis*, 10), in communion with the bishop, with Peter and under Peter. Through the priesthood of the bishop, the priesthood of the second order is incorporated in the apostolic structure of the Church. In this way priests, like the apostles, act as ambassadors of Christ (cf. 2 Cor 5:20). This is the basis of the missionary character of every priest.

Therefore, the ordained ministry arises with the Church and has in bishops, and in priests who are related to and

---

[34] Emphasis ours.

are in communion with them, a particular relation to the original ministry of the apostles—to which it truly "succeeds"—even though, with regard to the latter, it assumes different forms.

Consequently, the ordained priesthood ought not to be thought of as existing prior to the Church, because it is totally at the service of the Church. Nor should it be considered as posterior to the ecclesial community, as if the Church could be imagined as already established without this priesthood.

The relation of the priest to Jesus Christ, and in him to his Church, is found in the very being of the priest by virtue of his sacramental consecration/anointing and in his activity, that is, in his mission or ministry. In particular,

> the priest minister is the servant of Christ present in the Church as mystery, communion and mission. In virtue of his participation in the "anointing" and "mission" of Christ, the priest can continue Christ's prayer, word, sacrifice and salvific action in the Church. In this way, the priest is a servant of the Church as mystery because he actuates the Church's sacramental signs of the presence of the risen Christ. He is a servant of the Church as communion because—in union with the bishop and closely related to the presbyterate—he builds up the unity of the Church community in the harmony of diverse vocations, charisms and services. Finally, the priest is a servant to the Church as mission because he makes the community a herald and witness of the Gospel.

Thus, by his very nature and sacramental mission, the priest appears in the structure of the Church as a sign of the absolute priority and gratuitousness of the grace given to the Church by the risen Christ. Through the ministerial priesthood the Church becomes aware in faith that her being comes not from herself but from the grace of Christ in the Holy Spirit. The apostles and their successors, inasmuch as they exercise an authority which comes to them from Christ, the Head and Shepherd, are placed—with their ministry—in the forefront of the Church as a visible continuation and sacramental sign of Christ in his own position before the Church and the world, as the enduring and ever new source of salvation, he "who is head of the Church, his body, and is himself its savior" (Eph 5:23).[35]

Meditation

In accepting priestly ordination, the priest places himself totally at Christ's disposal at every moment. And so, for us priests, to put on Christ is to give ourselves entirely to Him as He gave Himself to us. This event is renewed during each Mass through the fact that we put on the liturgical vestments. Vesting solemnly, and not mechanically or distractedly, should be more than an external deed for us: Benedict XVI says that it is entering ever anew into the yes of our responsibility—into this "no longer I" of Baptism—which priestly ordination gives us in a new way and, at the same time, demands of us. The fact that we are at the altar, clothed in the

[35] John Paul II, Post-Synodal Apostolic Exhortation *Pastores dabo vobis* (March 25, 1992), nos. 14-16.

liturgical vestments, should immediately make visible to those present and to ourselves that we are there in the person of another. Priestly vestments are a profound, symbolic expression of what the priesthood signifies.

The act of putting them on was formerly accompanied by prayers that help us to understand better each element of priestly ministry, starting with the amice. In the past—and still in monastic orders—it was placed first on the head, like a sort of cowl, thus becoming a symbol of disciplining our senses and concentrating our thoughts; both of these are necessary for a correct and pious celebration of the Mass, experienced with recollection, reverence, and awe. Indeed, my thoughts must not wander here and there after the worries and expectations of my everyday life; my senses must not be attracted by anything inside the church that by chance might preoccupy my eyes, ears, and attention. My heart must be docile and open to the Word of God and be recollected in the prayer of the Church, so that my thoughts might receive their orientation from the words of the proclamation and of this prayer. And the eyes of my heart must be turned toward the Lord, Who is among us: this is what the *ars celebrandi* means—the correct way of celebrating. If I am with the Lord in this way and my attention is turned toward Him, then, by my attentive listening, my way of standing before Him, speaking, and acting, I will draw other persons also into intimate communion with Him.

Prayer texts that interpret the alb and the stole are along the same lines: The alb: its name means "white"; it symbolizes the purity and sanctity that are always required in order to celebrate the work of God, as Saint Benedict calls the liturgy. The alb and the stole recall the festive garment that the father in Saint Luke's parable gives to the prodigal son when he has come back home, dirty and in rags. When we approach the liturgy to act *in persona*

Christi, in the person of Christ, we all notice how far we are from Him; how there is dirt in our lives. He alone can give us the festive garment and make us holy and worthy to preside at His table, to be at His service. Thus, the prayers also recall the words of the book of Revelation, saying that the garments of the 144,000 elect had been washed and whitened in the blood of the Lamb. "Therefore are they before the throne of God, and serve him day and night within his temple" (Rev 7:14–15).

The chasuble: this is the outer garment that the priest puts on to celebrate Mass. It has its origin in a Roman cloak, the *paenula*, the same cloak that Saint Paul had forgotten in Troas at the house of Carpus (2 Tim 4:13). The chasuble is the vestment that totally covers the priest who celebrates Mass. It represents the yoke of the Lord Jesus, which has been placed on us in our capacity as priests. It recalls the words of Christ, Who invites us carry His yoke and to learn from Him, and tells us that He is "gentle and lowly in heart" (Mt 11:29). Wearing the chasuble means learning from Him how to submit with docility and for love of the Father's will; how we should humble ourselves and disappear in the presence of Jesus Christ, so that He alone may be visible. To wear the chasuble is to be ever ready to go to His school, so that He might teach us to be meek and humble of heart, as He is, and to love God and our neighbor as He does. It is absolutely inadequate and sad to celebrate the great Mystery of our faith while wearing only an alb and a stole. Every Eucharist is a solemnity, a feast, and at the same time the celebration of the Crucifixion of Jesus. Jesus had ascended to the altar of Golgotha solemnly with His noble, precious tunic. "The tunic was without seam, woven from top to bottom" (Jn 19:23). We, too, put on again the yoke of Jesus, His noble tunic, in ascending to the altar of sacrifice to die with Him. Mass is the most holy act, the principal and most important act of our priestly life.[36] It is an act that sanctifies us and configures us to Christ.

A great theologian and mystic, Father Philippon, just before his death, wrote the spiritual biography of a Mexican mother of a family who had died in 1937, Blessed María Concepción, known as Conchita, whose beatification ceremony was celebrated on May 4, 2019, at the Shrine of Our Lady of Guadalupe. Father Philippon records several things that Christ confided to this mother that seem to me to have distressing relevance. Here is how Blessed Conchita reports what she received as a private revelation:

> Of all men, Christ said, I singled out some who were to be mine, "other Christs," who would continue the mission that brought Me to earth, the mission of leading to my Father what had come from Him, souls that will glorify Him eternally. I could never finish telling you what priests are for Me: my hands, my laborers, my very Heart, and the center of countless souls. At the moment the world is making a wide breach in the hearts of priests, and you know how many vices accompany that formidable enemy. When the Holy Spirit leaves the heart of a priest, it is his ruin, because if anyone has not only the need but also the most imperative duty to live and to breathe the Holy Spirit, it is the priest. Woe to the priest who settles down into material things; he can consider himself lost. I want the love of my priests; I want the interior life; I want these consecrated souls to live in intimacy with Me. It is necessary to kindle once again the fire in my priests, and this will be done by the Holy Spirit alone.

[36] Pope Benedict XVI, Homily, Holy Thursday, April 5, 2007.

As I told you, even worse times for my Church will come, and She needs holy priests who will make her triumph over her enemies. I need an army of holy priests who have been transformed by Me. I need other Christs on earth, because my goal, for priests, is to complete their transformation into Me. The priest must continue in his ordinary life his transformation into Me which takes place in the Mass, so that this life becomes interior, spiritual, and divine.[37]

How could we not be joyful, given this divine call? Certainly it is demanding, but God gives us His grace. It is up to us to praise and thank Him every day for the wonders that He accomplishes in us.

[37] Marie-Michel Philippon, *Conchita: Journal spirituel d'une mère de famille* (Paris: Desclées de Brouwer, 1975). Translated from French.

V

Putting an End to Clericalism

Based on a meditation by Cardinal Jean-Marie Lustiger

Introduction

The spirit of the world is infiltrating the Church. Now, the spirit of the world is woven out of fear, jealousy, falsehood, the attraction of material riches, and the desire to dominate. In the Church we have seen rivalries and power plays spring up. This is probably what Saint Paul VI meant when he spoke about the smoke of Satan in the Church. I see one of its most terrible manifestations in the rivalry between the states of life. Clerics are jealous of the secular character of laypeople; they abandon the cassock and imitate laypeople slavishly in their attire. They want to engage in political action, which is properly the domain of the laity. Many of them publish writings not about the Word of God but about democracy, good government, peace and justice, and ecology. Some even speak in a very odd way about a "green Church." Similarly, laypeople are jealous of clerics. They want to imitate clerics, preside at liturgies, govern parishes, and preach during Sunday Mass. And now they are encouraging a vain, useless power struggle between women and men. Some women and some nuns want to be priests, and the priests hesitate to exercise their spiritual fatherhood. What is the source of so much confusion?

I think that a false and destructive idea has been introduced into the Church: that every responsibility, every state of life, is above all else a power or a right. Hence, the life of the Church as a whole is analyzed in terms of a power struggle and the balance of power. This thought structure, inherited from Marxism, was popularized through French Theory by American and European university circles. According to this hermeneutic, all of society is fundamentally a balance of power and domination. Hence, all behaviors are nothing but struggles to abolish or preserve structures of domination and privilege.

I think that clericalism is an attitude that feeds on this ulterior motive. It affects clerics as well as laypeople. It is a dangerous threat to the whole structure and to the members of the Church: from the pope through the priests down to the least of the laypeople. It is described as a struggle for power and domination: laymen "become clericalized" in order to seize the alleged power of the clerics. They demand "ministries," understood as external privileges, which the early Church and the first Christians who assisted Saint Paul never created or demanded. I wrote in *From the Depths of Our Hearts* that it was not necessary to "clericalize the laypeople" to give them their fair place in the Church, and I asked: "Would women not be respectable unless they were clerics? In the Church, is the clerical state the only way to exist and to have a place?"[38] I was particularly moved to read some time afterward similar words penned by Pope Francis, who declared in *Querida Amazonia*:

[38] Benedict XVI and Robert Cardinal Sarah, *From the Depths of Our Hearts*, trans. Michael J. Miller (San Francisco: Ignatius Press, 2019), 94.

This summons us to broaden our vision, lest we restrict our understanding of the Church to her functional structures. Such a reductionism would lead us to believe that women would be granted a greater status and participation in the Church only if they were admitted to Holy Orders. But that approach would in fact narrow our vision; it would lead us to clericalize women, diminish the great value of what they have already accomplished, and subtly make their indispensable contribution less effective.

Jesus Christ appears as the Spouse of the community that celebrates the Eucharist through the figure of a man who presides as a sign of the one Priest. This dialogue between the Spouse and his Bride, which arises in adoration and sanctifies the community, should not trap us in partial conceptions of power in the Church. The Lord chose to reveal his power and his love through two human faces: the face of his divine Son made man and the face of a creature, a woman, Mary. Women make their contribution to the Church in a way that is properly theirs, by making present the tender strength of Mary, the Mother. As a result, we do not limit ourselves to a functional approach, but enter instead into the inmost structure of the Church.[39]

This statement, which is so clear and so faithful to Tradition, ought to stop definitively all theological inquiry about a possibility of creating deaconesses in the Catholic Church. None of the persons who helped and supported Paul in his mission of evangelization ever expressed the desire to be instituted a minister. We should

---

[39] Francis, Post-Synodal Apostolic Exhortation, *Querida Amazonia* (February 2, 2020), nos. 100-101.

mention Aquila and his wife, Priscilla, who were outstanding collaborators of Paul in Corinth and Ephesus (Acts 18:18-19; 1 Cor 16:19), then in Rome (Rom 16:3; 2 Tim 4:19), or Epaphroditus (Phil 2:25) and Epaphras (Col 1:7; 4:12; Philem 23). We could also mention Apollos, originally from Alexandria, a learned man, well versed in the Scriptures, who had had great success in Corinth and Ephesus (Acts 18:24-28; 1 Cor 1:12; 3:4-6; Tit 3:13). Saint Luke points out, besides the Twelve who were with Jesus, the presence of women: Mary, called Magdalene; Joanna, wife of Chuza, Herod's steward; Susanna; "and many others who provided for them out of their means" (Lk 8:1-9; Mt 27:55; Mk 15:41). None of these persons claimed a ministry. They all participated generously, out of love, in the mission of Jesus. For centuries, catechists have participated in the work of missionaries with heroic, humble zeal without demanding that someone give them a ministerial responsibility. They never wished to be clericalized. They were always great witnesses and wonderful fathers and mothers of families.

Clericalism is an attitude that transforms a state of life, a ministry, or a responsibility into private property and a stepping-stone for someone with an ego complex. Pope Francis calls this self-referentiality. Whereas each state of life is a specific form of referring to the mystery of Christ and of identifying with one aspect of this mystery, clericalism appropriates the missions that they confer and makes them an instrument of power.

Vatican II has the ingenious and prophetic intention of highlighting the complementarity among the states of life and not their competition or aggressive rivalry. It is necessary to reread *Lumen gentium*, which describes the multiple forms of practicing holiness:

The forms and tasks of life are many but holiness is one—that sanctity which is cultivated by all who act under

God's Spirit and, obeying the Father's voice and adoring God the Father in spirit and in truth, follow Christ, poor, humble and cross-bearing, that they may deserve to be partakers of his glory. Each one, however, according to his own gifts and duties must steadfastly advance along the way of a living faith, which arouses hope and works through love.[40]

It is time to set aside the false logic of competition. "By reason of their special vocation it belongs to the laity to seek the kingdom of God by engaging in temporal affairs and directing them according to God's will."[41] The vocation belonging to consecrated religious is to be a prophetic reminder that the world cannot be transformed and offered to God without the radical message of the Gospel and the spirit of the Beatitudes. The vocation belonging to priests is to represent Christ the Shepherd sacramentally in the midst of His people, principally by the administering of the sacraments, the preaching of the gospel, and the service of authority, but also by their whole lives. The Church is not a place of power but of service. I will say it again: many laypeople are more competent and better educated than clerics in theology or in pastoral ministry. But they will never be able to "take the place of Christ the Shepherd and to act in his person."

Let us not forget that Baptism and Confirmation mark the soul with a sacramental character that gives persons a spiritual identity. It is up to baptized and confirmed laypeople to make present in the secular world the mystery of our adoption as children of God and witnesses of His Word. They must fight to establish the Kingdom of God in the world and not fritter away their energies

---

[40] *Lumen gentium* 41.
[41] *Lumen gentium* 31.

in order to enjoy some function within the Church. It is up to married laypeople to make present sacramentally the mystery of the nuptials of Christ and the Church by living out their conjugal love faithfully and in an exemplary fashion. It is up to religious and consecrated persons to witness to the radical nature of evangelical life and to the eschatological call to holiness. We need one another. We advance shoulder to shoulder; we help one another along the way of holiness.

Sometimes you hear people say that it is necessary to decentralize the exercise of authority and the ordained ministry. Here and there, it is said that government in the Church can be done just as well by men and women, by laymen and priests and bishops. Such formulas are terribly ambiguous and destructive, undermining the hierarchical structure of the Church as it was willed and organized by Jesus Christ Himself. Of course there are laypeople, men and women, who are more competent in communication, management, and government techniques than priests are. They should be appointed to the advisory roles that belong to them as experts. But in the strict sense, government in the Church is not in the first place a kind of expertise but a presence of Christ, the Servant and Shepherd. This is why the function of government can never be exercised in the Church by anyone but an ordained minister. Christians want to be governed by Christ and not by an expert. Because priests make Christ the Shepherd and Servant present sacramentally, they must govern not by exercising human domination but by prolonging the work of the Good Shepherd. Sometimes they are not up to their mission, but nevertheless this responsibility of government is entrusted to them by virtue of their ordination, which configures them to the Good Shepherd.

Once again, this does not diminish the need to utilize the competence and excellence of lay men and women. No decision should be made without consulting truly competent persons. But only a minister configured to the Good Shepherd can make decisions regarding the Church without authority turning into the power of domination in a human way.

Therefore, it is time to stop interpreting authority in the Church as a power or a form of oppression. It is, through and through, ministerial, because it is always a service rendered by the clerics to the entire Body. Consequently, it is accepted in a spirit of service, as Jesus taught the first twelve priests when He washed their feet. It is also accepted by priests who know their vocation and want to be instruments of the Good Shepherd and not tyrants.

Cardinal Jean-Marie Lustiger, who was archbishop of Paris from January 31, 1981, to February 11, 2005, clearly sums this up. This great servant of the Church was of Jewish origin. His conversion to Christ confirmed in him a deep sense of the unity and the dignity of the people of God. In his mission as a bishop, he had the genius and the talent to put the competencies belonging to each person, whether cleric or layman, at the service of the proclamation of the gospel. He was able to apply all the insights of Vatican Council II.

Cardinal Jean-Marie Lustiger, "The Vocation of Priests" (excerpts)

The body of pronouncements by John Paul II on the subject of priests, consecrated life, and the vocation of the baptized—therefore including the laity—covers thousands of pages. I would like to try here to highlight their logic and their originality, to understand their "economy" in the sense of the word as used by the Fathers [of the Church] to describe the economy of salvation in which the Trinitarian mystery is revealed to us. Beyond their diversity, one finds in them the great challenges of the life of the Church at the end of the twentieth centry and a coherent, structured response that draws its strength from the mystery of Christ....

On this subject [of priests], what was the general outlook of twenty-five years ago, when John Paul II pronounced his first words in public: "Do not be afraid! Open wide the doors to Christ"?...

The new Pope had a very precise knowledge of this. Seven years before, as Archbishop of Krakow, he had participated in the Second Ordinary Synod of Bishops held in Rome from 30 September to 6 November 1971, which dealt with the priestly ministry and justice in the world. Newspapers announced that the bishops would ask the Holy Father to ordain married *viri probati* [men of proven character]. Many suggested banishing the word "priesthood" in favour of "presbyteral ministry."

The outcome of the 1971 Synod is well known. Pope Paul VI bravely resisted such pressure. Was not the beatification of Father Maximilian Maria Kolbe as a "Catholic priest" his answer to these questions that downplayed the figure of presbyteral priesthood? In any case, the problems and the crisis I have just mentioned had put down lasting roots in the developed West.

Those who are old enough to have lived through this period will not have forgotten the intensity of the crisis in the 1970s, nor the questions posed by the desertions that increased and the drop in the number of candidates for seminaries.

Had the teaching of Vatican II really been understood at that time? Be that as it may, the problems of the Church were perceived by public opinion from an organizational or sociopolitical angle rather than from a theological or mystical one. In retrospect, one can recognize in them the symmetrical influences of Marxism and a certain liberalism. The former led to a conception of all things in terms of a power relationship. The latter was an invitation to consider all things in an administrative perspective and to promote individual freedom.

Obedience, poverty, chastity, and lastly the very nature of the priesthood and vocations, including the baptismal vocation of the laity, were obviously contested when reasoning according to [the criteria of] viability, power relationships or power sharing, and social recognition, whose only gauge is money, etc. Sociology was in the limelight; anthropology in its various branches seemed to defy the traditional teaching on sex, whereas history served to demonstrate the absolute relativity of ecclesiastical celibacy.

In short, three ideas obfuscated the spiritual and sacramental realities of presbyteral priesthood and of both the religious and baptismal vocation:

Firstly, the sacramental reality of the priesthood had to give way before the functionality of the ministerial tasks which, it seemed, could be carried out without ordination. This is what certain people have called "desacerdotalization."

Then, the dialectics of power led to the desire to entrust the latter to the democratic assembly of the faithful. This went by the name of "declericalization."

Lastly, the abolition of celibacy was supposed to complete the "secularization" of a Christianity considered too tied to an out-of-date culture.

Nevertheless, Vatican II had foreseen these difficulties. As *Gaudium et spes* proclaimed, "Ours is a new age of history with critical and swift upheavals spreading gradually to all corners of the earth.... We are entitled then to speak of a real social and cultural transformation whose repercussions are felt too on the religious level" (4, 2). But the intuitions of the Council in order to face this situation had yet to be fully implemented....

In 1978, how was the new Pope going to answer the questions that Paul VI had asked in 1971? Along what paths would he lead the Church of Christ over which he now had to watch?...

Ten years after the inauguration of his Pontificate, the three Post-Synodal Apostolic Exhortations began to appear. They were dedicated, respectively, to vocations, that is, to our subject: to the laity (*Christifideles laici*) in 1988, to priests (*Pastores dabo vobis*) in 1992, and to men and women religious (*Vita consecrata*) in 1996.

This group of three Encyclicals, followed by three Apostolic Exhortations, deploys a spiritual teaching [*pédagogie*] whose coherence is amazing.... And [the Pope's] steadfast aim is even more striking if one takes into account the circumstances and events that arose to hinder his development of it.

In a certain way the Pope establishes the foundation of the commitments of men and women in our time as they follow Christ, whether they are priests, consecrated religious, or laypersons, by placing them in the economy of salvation: at the end of this Advent, the person discovers himself in his inalienable dignity, which is his participation in the priesthood of Christ....

Indeed, in his teaching John Paul II focused first of all on what is at the root of the different states of life and the various missions in the Church, in other words, the mystery of Christ. It was certainly quite a radical reversal of outlook. For the Pope it was a matter of taking up the challenges of new times, of evaluating the real needs, and providing responses to them, no longer taking politics, sociology, or anthropology as criteria, but addressing the human being, wounded and redeemed, such as faith grants us to see and to love. This realism of faith sets people free from the prison of ideologies.

In *Gift and Mystery*, we read: "After I was elected Pope, my first spiritual impulse was to turn to Christ the Redeemer. This was the origin of the Encyclical Letter *Redemptor hominis*.... I see ever more clearly the close link between the message of that Encyclical and everything that is found in the heart of man through his sharing in Christ's priesthood."[42]

In other words, Redemption is not only what makes man intelligible to himself despite his contradictions and nihilistic or suicidal temptations. By enabling the human being to understand how much God loves him or her, the person begins to appreciate his infinite dignity, which requires an immediate and concrete union with Christ's sacrifice. Every Christian vocation finds in this its meaning and content, which are truly priestly....

Herein we have, of course, an essential orientation for this participation in the divine life that is the response to any vocation....

---

[42] Pope John Paul II, *Gift and Mystery: On the Fiftieth Anniversary of My Priestly Ordination* (New York: Doubleday, 1996), 82.

For Eternity

Today we can clearly perceive how the Pope wanted the 1971 Synod of Bishops to be resumed, starting from scratch. He required the three new Synods—first on the vocation of laypeople, then on the formation of priests, and lastly on the consecrated life—to formulate the appropriate answers....

Furthermore, the order of the three Synods is significant: to begin with, the laity sheds light on the universal vocation to holiness of the priestly People. Likewise, with laypersons, the Synod revisited *Gaudium et spes* as well as *Lumen gentium* and spelled out the mission of the Church of our time. The ministerial priesthood, the theme of the next Synod, suddenly appeared clearly as the means by which Christ wanted to make the holy People live; the radical call to holiness casts a prophetic light on the "special fittingness" of priestly celibacy. It must be considered consistent with the consecrated life, which signifies prophetically the destiny of humanity, whose eschatological anticipation it is here and now.

The logic of the three Apostolic Exhortations in the light of the three great Encyclicals of the beginning of the Pontificate develops from the concept of the priesthood which is itself inherent in the Redemption: "Christ is a priest because He is the Redeemer of the world," we read in *Gift and Mystery*.[43] The intuitions and memories given to us in this valuable text will once again be able to serve us as a guide or counterpoint to illumine or condense various aspects of vocations through their diversity and their theological and mystical unity.

[43] Pope John Paul II, *Gift and Mystery*, 82.

The mystery of the Redeemer offers man the understanding of his own condition: Christ reveals to humanity
that it is both wounded and loved. Christ's essentially
priestly immolation of Himself redeems human beings
from evil by giving them forgiveness for their sins. As a
priestly offering, it necessarily has a sacrificial dimension in
which, as John Paul II repeats at every opportunity, quoting
chapter 7 of the Letter to the Hebrews, Jesus is not content
with interceding because, as the "perfect High Priest," He
offers Himself as a "spotless victim." His Resurrection does
not only mean that His sacrifice is pleasing. In a sense, by
showing solidarity to the very end with humanity disfigured
by sin, in His obedience He fulfills the love that unites
Him to His Father from all eternity. On Easter morning,
He demonstrates that this love, which is the very life of
humanity, is victorious over death.

For men and women, salvation consists in offering
themselves in turn to the Father, united with Christ,
through the power of the Spirit, so as to make their own
contribution to spreading and sharing this mercy. The
Christian is in a certain way incorporated into Christ to
be associated with His priestly and redemptive action. To
this extent it is truly correct, following Vatican II, to speak
of the "common priesthood of all the baptized." ...

The Pope explains that "the priest, as steward of 'the
mysteries of God,' is at the service of the common priesthood of the faithful." We can see here that John Paul II
has powerfully renewed the approach to the roles, at the
same time very distinct and interdependent, of priests and
laypeople. He has likewise insisted on the fact that the
ecclesial mission of the lay faithful has its source in their

priestly dignity and flows into their temporal tasks. He has also shown that the immediate purpose of the ordained ministries is to enable this vocation of every baptized person to be fulfilled.

Here each word has an importance of its own. The common priesthood is not the origin of the presbyteral priesthood. The latter is at the service of the former but does not derive from it. The reason for this, as the Pope points out in *Gift and Mystery*, is that "the priesthood, in its deepest reality, is the priesthood of Christ,"[44] and of no one else.

It remains to legitimize the distinction and complementarity of these two aspects or levels of the one priesthood. Among other things, this is what the Synod of 1990 and the Apostolic Exhortation *Pastores dabo vobis*, published sixteen months later in 1992, set out to do. It should not be forgotten that this Synod first focused on the formation of priests. Nonetheless, the final text signed by the Pope is one of the longest papal documents ever to be published (226 pages in the original edition), and the issues are thoroughly treated, going back to the most exalted and decisive principles.

It is out of the question, therefore, to list here all the resources offered by *Pastores dabo vobis*. However, as regards what concerns us here, we will be able once again to find a significant echo of them in *Gift and Mystery*. John Paul II writes, "... While the Second Vatican Council speaks of the *universal* call to holiness, in the case of the priest we must speak of a *special* call to holiness. Christ needs holy priests! Today's world demands holy priests! Only a holy priest can become, in an increasingly secularized world, a resounding witness to

[44] Pope John Paul II, *Gift and Mystery*, 75.

Christ and his Gospel. And only thus can a priest become a guide for men and women and a teacher of holiness. People, especially the young, are looking for such guides."[45]

The priest does not choose this special holiness on his own, although he commits his freedom to it: he is called, ordained, and consecrated to it, in order to speak and act *in persona Christi*. This vocation, this mission, cannot be given to him by anyone other than Jesus Himself, and it requires a specific gift of the Holy Spirit....

John Paul II insists on two situations in which the priest "offers his humanity to Christ, so that Christ may use him as an instrument of salvation, making him as it were into another Christ."[46]

First comes the celebration of Mass. "In our world, is there any greater fulfillment of our humanity than to be able to re-present every day *in persona Christi* the redemptive sacrifice, the same sacrifice which Christ offered on the Cross?" the Pope asks. "In this sacrifice, on the one hand, the very mystery of the Trinity is present in the most profound way, and, on the other hand, the entire created universe is 'united' [*récapitulé*: cf. Eph 1:10]."[47]

Secondly, there is what the Pope calls "the ministry of mercy." "The priest," he stresses, "is the witness and instrument of divine mercy! How important in his life is the ministry of the confessional! It is in the confessional that his spiritual fatherhood is realized in the fullest way."[48]

---

[45] Pope John Paul II, *Gift and Mystery*, 89.
[46] Pope John Paul II, *Gift and Mystery*, 73.
[47] Pope John Paul II, *Gift and Mystery*, 73.
[48] Pope John Paul II, *Gift and Mystery*, 86.

Here we are permitted to see in action the relationship between fatherhood and mercy, mentioned above in the reference to the Encyclical on the heavenly Father. In its paternal dimension the priesthood implies, as it were, a "distance" or, if you like, a distinction, a differentiation, a "setting aside." ... It is in this perspective, among others, that we can understand the "special" character of holiness to which the priest is expressly called.

The vocation to the priesthood takes the very precise form that John Paul II describes in *Gift and Mystery*, explaining that his ministry commits him "to a way of life inspired by the radicalism of the Gospel. This explains his particular need to live in the spirit of the evangelical counsels of chastity, poverty and obedience."[49]

The indissoluble bond between the priesthood and sacrifice justifies such a requirement. Remembering his own ordination, the Holy Father singles out the profound meaning of one of the rites of the sacrament. The future priest, he writes, "prostrates himself completely and rests his forehead on the church floor, indicating in this way his *complete willingness to undertake the ministry* being entrusted to him."[50] And he comments: "In lying prostrate on the floor in the form of a cross before one's ordination, in accepting in one's own life—like Peter—the cross of Christ and becoming with the Apostle a 'floor' for our brothers and sisters, one finds the ultimate meaning of all priestly spirituality."[51]

[49] Pope John Paul II, *Gift and Mystery*, 88.
[50] Pope John Paul II, *Gift and Mystery*, 44–45.
[51] Pope John Paul II, *Gift and Mystery*, 46.

The Pope explains clearly that there is no ensuing injury to the person. On the contrary, the "young man, hearing the words 'Follow me!', can give up everything for Christ, in the certainty that if he follows this path he will find complete personal fulfillment."[52]

But the evangelical counsels lead us almost naturally to the third Synod of Bishops, which addressed vocations in 1994, with concern for the religious life, and to the Apostolic Exhortation *Vita consecrata*, again, sixteen months later, in 1996.

John Paul II concludes by stressing, among other things, a difficulty he has come across at the end of the twentieth century, not only within a number of Religious Orders but also throughout the Church: the temptation to evaluate everything by the utilitarian criteria of society. The consecrated life, the Pope responded, obeys other laws, and in particular that of the gift, both inherent in the human condition and confirmed by the Incarnation and the Cross. Lives that are totally devoted to God, with no prospect of "gratification" here on earth, help contemporary culture once again to call itself into question. They are also witnesses in this world to the coming of the Kingdom of God that has already begun.

But the "radicalism of the Gospel" still has a "motivating" role in the Church, not only by virtue of the many services rendered by religious men and women, but especially through the examples and models of holiness offered by priests and baptized laypersons who have taken vows. This revitalizes the entire People of God, the clergy as well as the faithful....

Consecrated life in some way mirrors or integrates and then reflects back the freedom and superabundance of

[52] Pope John Paul II, *Gift and Mystery*, 73.

God's gifts, without denying any of those that have already been irreversibly dispensed. On the contrary, it stimulates their assimilation by means of the constantly renewed variety and riches of vocations and commitments.

This perspective easily enables one to avoid the polemics that arose after the publication of *Vita consecrata*, on the translation of the Latin word *praecellens*. Was it necessary to infer that the religious state of men and women religious is "objectively superior" to other states of life?

The question, in truth, just as often arises regarding the relationship between the clergy and the faithful. That the holiness to which the priest is called has something "special" about it takes nothing from the authentic perfection to which laypeople are also called.

The very existence of consecrated life illustrates the same logic of the gratuitous and organic coherence which already expresses the complementarity between the "common priesthood" and the presbyteral priesthood, without the possibility of giving either one greater importance. "Gospel radicalism" has been shown to work in the same kind of interdependence, in need of the same mystical order for the benefit of the whole People of God and of the world whose Saviour is Christ.

Many lessons can be learned from the picture that has just been sketched.... In the first place, John Paul II has directly and vigorously grappled with the difficulties the Church has met in the last third of the twentieth century. He has not overlooked anything, therefore, in either our trials or our temptations. But he has done so by firmly shifting the problem.

He asks us to replace a reflection in terms of power over the institutions with a renewed perception of the drama of the human condition, deciphered in the light of the mystery at the heart of the Christian faith: the Redemption.

In other words, the Pope has been able to refocus everything on Christ without the fear of not being "part of the times in which he lives." ...

John Paul II therefore writes:

> I am convinced that a priest, committed as he is to this necessary pastoral renewal, should at the same time have no fear of being "behind the times," because the human "today" of every priest is included in the "today" of Christ the Redeemer. For every priest, in every age, the greatest task is each day to discover his own priestly "today" in the "today" of Christ to which the Letter to the Hebrews refers (13:8). "... Jesus Christ is the same yesterday and today and for ever."[53]

Meditation

As Dom Hugh Gilbert, O.S.B., wrote in his book *Unfolding the Mystery*:

> The Eucharist teaches us about ourselves and the Eucharist means standing at the altar. It is *the* place for Christians

---

[53] Cardinal Jean-Marie Lustiger, "The Vocation of Priests," conference given in Rome for the opening of the Congress of Cardinals and Presidents of Episcopal Conferences, meeting on the occasion of the twenty-fifth anniversary of the Pontificate of John Paul II, October 15-18, 2003. English translation from *L'Osservatore Romano*, weekly edition in English, December 17/24, 2003, p. 15, slightly emended.

to be: their redemption *and* their vocation.... If we stand at the altar, it is because we have been baptized. And if we have been baptized, we have been attached to the Cross. Attachment to the Cross means at once a breaking with sin and a widening of the heart ... by letting it be pierced. Standing at the altar, for the priest as well as for the lay faithful, means offering oneself as a burnt-offering to God, handing oneself over to God totally.... Standing at the altar really means to be conformed, to be identified with Christ, who by his death offers himself to God the Father, and to re-consecrate the world to the Lord of the universe.[54]

"For every high priest chosen from among men is appointed to act on behalf of men in relation to God" (Heb 5:1). And although he himself is wrapped in the same infirmities, needing the divine mercy and forgiveness as much as others, and even more, to him nevertheless is entrusted a power greater than himself, greater than the world, and greater than all the distinctions that the world can confer on a human being—a power that comes to him from Christ. Thus, Saint John Vianney, the Curé of Ars, could say that "the priest is a man who takes the place of God, a man who is vested with all the powers of God." And he adds: "Oh! What a great thing the priest is! If he understood it he would die. God obeys him: he says two words and Our Lord descends from Heaven at his voice and shuts himself into a little host."[55]

The Catholic Church teaches that only a validly consecrated priest can make the bodily Presence of Christ and of His redeeming

[54] Dom Hugh Gilbert, O.S.B., *Unfolding the Mystery* (Herefordshire: Gracewing Publishing, 2007), 24–25, 27–28 [the second excerpt was translated from French].

[55] Nodet, *Jean-Marie Vianney*.

sacrifice come down and dwell in our midst, when, in the name of Christ's omnipotence, he pronounces the transubstantiating words spoken at the Last Supper.

We priests are men who have been called. The story of our priesthood starts with a call from God, as it happened for the Apostles.

> And passing along by the Sea of Galilee, he saw Simon and Andrew the brother of Simon casting a net in the sea; for they were fishermen. And Jesus said to them, "Follow me and I will make you become fishers of men." And immediately they left their nets and followed him. And going on a little farther, he saw James the son of Zebedee and John his brother, who were in their boat mending the nets. And immediately he called them; and they left their father Zebedee in the boat with the hired servants, and followed him. (Mk 1:16–20)

Therefore, God, Jesus, is the One Who takes the initiative; He is the One Who takes the first step and comes to us. "You did not choose me, but I chose you" (Jn 15:16). We should meditate often on this very special way in which God looks at us, so that we can remain faithful to the grace of our priesthood.

Whom does Jesus choose? He does not seem to look at the noble origins, the brilliant intellectual qualifications, or the social condition of His chosen followers.

> God chose what is foolish in the world to shame the wise, God chose what is weak in the world to shame the strong, God chose what is low and despised in the world, even things that are not, to bring to nothing things that are, so that no flesh might boast in the presence of God. (1 Cor 1:27–29)

Nor does He favor those who are strong-willed, moved by a superficial enthusiasm (Mt 8:19-22). One thing is certain: we are called by Christ, by God. He is the one who "set us apart before we were born and called us through his grace" (see Gal 1:15). This means that we are loved immensely by Christ, loved by God. We have been taken away from the world and given to Him, set apart for God and for Him alone.

Do we really think about this? To be a priest: what an extraordinary gift given to humanity! Do we appreciate the immense privilege and the extraordinary gift that have thus been given to us? In reality, the vocation to the priesthood is a sign of predilection on the part of Him Who, by choosing us from among so many brothers who are more intelligent, more worthy, and holier than we are, called us to share in a very special way in His friendship and in His priesthood. And so our priestly being is therefore nothing less than a new and radical way of being configured to Christ and more intimately united to Him. "No longer do I call you servants, for the servant does not know what his master is doing; but I have called you friends, for all that I have heard from my Father I have made known to you" (Jn 15:15). Our call to the priesthood, by marking the most exalted moment in the use of our free will, caused the great, irreversible choice in our lives, and therefore the happiest, noblest, most beautiful page in the story of our human experience. The complete fulfillment of our life and our happiness lie in never disappointing God by despising or negligently and thoughtlessly receiving the priceless treasure of priestly grace.

VI

Vocation to Prayer

Based on a meditation by Saint Bernard of Clairvaux

Introduction

It is reinvigorating to reread Saint Bernard! Here is a man capable of great gentleness and sweet poetry when he addresses the Virgin Mary. And yet here is a priest capable of forcefully and firmly denouncing the sins of his contemporaries. In his letter *De consideratione*, Saint Bernard writes to Pope Eugene III, who had been a Cistercian monk and therefore his disciple and pupil. The sensible, sound advice that he gives him is still valuable for every priest today. They even have an odd relevance. Indeed, Bernard of Clairvaux, in the twelfth century, comes at the conclusion of what is called in Church history the Gregorian reform. This movement during the tenth, eleventh, and twelfth centuries aimed to liberate the Church from the influence of the secular authorities. By interfering in Church government and ecclesiastical appointments, the political authorities had ended up producing a genuinely decadent clergy. Priests with concubines, engaged in commerce or political affairs, had become common. The Gregorian reform is characterized by the desire to rediscover the Church of the time of the Acts of the Apostles. This movement did not rely at first on institutional reforms but on the renewal of the holiness of priests.

Do we not need a similar reform today? Do we not need a new Gregorian reform? Indeed, the secular authority of the world has once again seized power in the Church. We are not talking about the political authorities this time but about the cultural authorities. There is indeed a new battle between the priesthood and the empire. But the empire now is the relativistic, hedonistic, and consumerist culture that has infiltrated everywhere. It is time to drive it out because it cannot be reconciled with the gospel. It is time to win back the freedom of our hearts from the worldly dictates that proclaim the kingdom of triumphant matter and egotistical pride. We must claim the glory of our divine King, whose attributes are the Cross and the humility of the manger. The same causes produce the same effects: as in the Middle Ages, the infiltration of the world into the Church gives rise to sexual and financial scandals among priests and spawns abuses of authority and a deadly spiritual aridity.

As in the twelfth century, we must take measures to apply a thoroughgoing treatment, a radical purification. As Pope Saint John Paul II reminds us:

> Through the Spirit, Jesus belongs totally and exclusively to God and shares in the infinite holiness of God, who calls him, chooses him and sends him forth. In this way the Spirit of the Lord is revealed as the source of holiness and of the call to holiness.
>
> The Council's statement that "all Christians in any state or walk of life are called to the fullness of Christian life and to the perfection of charity" applies in a special way to priests. They are called not only because they have been baptized, but also and specifically because they are priests,

that is, under a new title and in new and different ways deriving from the sacrament of Holy Orders.[56]

Saint Bernard gives us a key with which to liberate the priest from the chains of worldly culture: prayer. Actually, the priest has a vocation to prayer. He is not just obliged to pray the hours of the breviary. He is called by God, as a priest, to pray for all and in the name of all. Prayer is not the specific work of monks alone. It is an essential and principal part of the priestly vocation.

As Saint Bernard superbly puts it: "Since you are all things to all men, be that for yourselves too." A priest who does not pray is living in an illusion of generosity and self-giving. The time that a priest dedicates to prayer is not time taken from others. On the contrary, by dedicating time to God, the priest makes himself even more available so as to give himself more generously. Certainly, it is sometimes difficult to find the time in the midst of so many demands. But we have to believe that, without prayer, all our agitation is in vain. It runs the risk of turning into social action rather than priestly ministry. The faithful need to see us praying at great length. They intuitively know that a priest who prays is a priest who loves them. On the contrary, a priest who stops praying inevitably falls into self-deception, loses the sense of sure, true doctrine, and doubts himself. How many times have we said about a priest who was leaving the ministry in tragic circumstances: "He had stopped praying a long time ago!" This is an urgent matter. The reform of the clergy starts with a reform of the interior life of priests. It is time to rediscover our vocation to prayer.

What does it mean to pray? To answer this vital question, we turn to the writings of Saint Thérèse of the Child Jesus, who speaks about prayer in the following terms:

[56] John Paul II, *Pastores dabo vobis* 19.

For me, prayer is a surge of the heart; it is a simple look turned toward heaven, it is a cry of recognition and of love, embracing both trial and joy. It is a simple glance directed to heaven, it is something great, supernatural, which expands my soul and unites me to Jesus.... Sometimes when I am in such a state of spiritual dryness that not a single good thought occurs to me, I say very slowly the "Our Father," or the "Hail Mary," and these prayers suffice to take me out of myself. They feed my soul much more than if I had recited them hastily a hundred times.[57]

To pray, therefore, is not to recite prayers or one's breviary hastily and, so to speak, mechanically. To pray is to prostrate oneself before God in a silence of awe and wonder, to adore Him and to tell Him that we love Him, to thank Him for all His benefits, to sing His glory and exalt His saving power on behalf of mankind. To pray is to devote time to contemplating God, looking at Him and letting Him look at me. In our priestly ministry, we run the serious risk of activism, "the heresy of works," the worldly mentality that does not admit that a significant part of our time each day should be devoted to silent prayer and standing in God's presence. We no longer see the usefulness of entire lives devoted exclusively to prayer and sacrifice so as to make the wellsprings of the deep life of sanctity flow abundantly in the Church. Activism in priestly life is the result of a deep-seated tendency to deny in practice the action of the Holy Spirit in the soul and in the Church. Activism weakens our whole spiritual life, makes the apostolate fruitless—even though it may be decked out in brilliant external success—and may lead to lamentable moral and spiritual

---

[57] Thérèse of the Child Jesus, Manuscript C, fol. 25.

catastrophes. To spare us such dangers, Saint John of the Cross exhorts us to prayer and reflection:

> Let those men of zeal, who think by their preaching and exterior works to convert the world, consider that they would be much more edifying to the Church, and more pleasing to God—setting aside the good example they would give—if they would spend at least one half their time in prayer.... To act otherwise is to beat the air, to do little more than nothing, sometimes nothing and occasionally even mischief ... for God may give up such persons to vanity, so that they may seem to have done something, when in reality their outward occupations bear no fruit; for it is quite certain that good works cannot be done but in the power of God.[58]

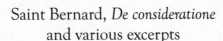

Saint Bernard, *De consideratione* and various excerpts

Letter 42 of Saint Bernard, or "Treatise to Henry, Archbishop of Sens, on the Morals and Duties of Bishops"

But whom do you wish to please, O priest of the Most-High? The world, or God? If the world, then why did you become a priest?... If you want to please the world, I ask you why you received priestly ordination; you know

---

[58] John of the Cross, *Spiritual Canticle of the Soul and the Bridegroom Christ*, trans. David Lewis, with corrections and an introduction by Benedict Zimmermann, O.C.D. (Grand Rapids, MI: Christian Classics Ethereal Library, 2000), stanza XXVIII, 3.

very well that one cannot serve two masters at the same time.... And doesn't the Apostle say: "If I were still pleasing men, I should not be a servant of Christ" (Gal 1:10)? Thus, by wishing to please men, you would be unable to please God; but if you do not please him at all, how will you gain his favor?... Finally, if you are a priest, you are a pastor, and the people are your flock; now should there be no difference between the sheep and the shepherd who leads them? If the one who pastures me, a mere sheep, walks like me with his eyes and body bent down toward the ground, entirely preoccupied with filling his belly while his soul is empty, what distinguishes him from me? Woe to the flock if the wolf comes to swoop down on them, for there will be no one to notice him before he arrives, to confront him and fight to keep him from his prey. Is it right that the pastor, like his flock, should be occupied solely with satisfying his sensual appetites, the slave of base thoughts, eager for earthly goods, instead of walking with his head high and uplifted, since man's lot is to look to heaven, to seek and taste the things on high, and not those of this world?[59]

On Conversion, XIX

The men whom the Heavenly Father calls the pure of heart are those who, instead of seeking their own interests, have in view only those of Jesus Christ and do not demand at

---

[59] Bernard de Clairvaux, *Lettre 42 de saint Bernard, ou "Traité à Henri, archevêque de Sens, sur les moeurs et les devoirs des évêques,"* in: *Oeuvres complètes*, French translation by Father Charpentier, vol. I (Paris, 1866).

all what is useful for them, but what is useful for everyone. "Peter, do you love me?" the Savior of the world asked. "Lord, you know that I love you." "Feed my sheep," the Divine Master replied (Jn 21:15–17). How could he have entrusted his beloved sheep to a shepherd who did not love the Master himself at all?... Woe to the unfaithful ministers who, when they themselves are not yet reconciled, take responsibility for reconciling others, as men who are just in every respect could do! Woe to those children of wrath who set themselves up as ministers of mercy! Woe to those children of wrath who have the audacity to lay claim to the title and rank that belong only to the peacemakers! Woe to those children of wrath who disguise themselves as faithful mediators of peace in order to fatten themselves on the sins of the people!... For with such impudence we see men who have never heard the Word of the Lord inviting them to recollect themselves, or who, having heard it, have fled like Adam to hide among thick foliage and to usurp the rank and the offices of peaceful men and of the true children of God. And so to this day they have not stopped doing evil; they still drag behind them bits of the net in which they were ensnared; they still have not opened their eyes to their poverty; on the contrary, each one says, "I am rich, I have prospered, and I need nothing," whereas he is "wretched, pitiable, poor, blind, and naked" (Rev 3:17). They possess nothing of the spirit of gentleness that is so necessary in order to rebuke sinners, while watching over oneself, so as not to fall in turn into temptation.[60]

[60] Bernard of Clairvaux, *Sermon ou livre de saint Bernard abbé aux prêtres sur la conversion*, in *Oeuvres completes*.

For Eternity

*"One must not take care of others
to the point of neglecting oneself"*

On Consideration, Book 1

If you give all your life and all your wisdom to action, and nothing to prayer [= consideration], do I praise you? In this I praise you not. I suppose no one would who has heard Solomon's words, "He that hath little business shall become wise" (Sir 37:25). Action itself certainly does not fare well unless preceded by prayer.

If you wish to belong altogether to other people, like him who was made all things to all men, I praise your humanity, but only on condition that it be complete. But how can it be complete if you yourself are left out? You, too, are a man. So then, in order that your humanity may be entire and complete, let your bosom, which receives all, find room for yourself also. Otherwise, according to the word of the Lord, what does it profit you if you gain the whole world and lose your own self?

Wherefore, though all possess you, take care that you are one among them. Why are you alone defrauded of your reward? How long will you be a wind that passeth away and cometh not again? Will the time never come when you will in turn receive yourself among the rest? You are a debtor both to the wise and to the foolish; and are you the only one to whom you deny yourself? Wise and foolish, bond and free, rich and poor, male and female, old and young, cleric and layman, righteous and wicked, all alike share in you, all drink at the public fountain of your heart; and will you stand apart and thirst? If he is cursed who impairs his inheritance, what are we to say of him who strips himself of it altogether? By all means let your waters stream down into the streets; let men and flocks and herds drink thereof, nay, let the servants of Abraham give drink even to the camels; but among the rest do you yourself drink of the water of your own well. "Let not a stranger," saith the Scripture, "drink thereat" (Prov 5:17). Are you a stranger? To whom are you not a stranger, if you are one to yourself? In short, if a man is bad to himself, to whom is he good? (Sir 14:5). So remember, I do not say always, I do not say often, but at least sometimes, to restore yourself to yourself. Among the many, or at all events after the many, do you also make use of yourself....

If I wished to speak strongly, or with perfect sincerity say all that is right, I should say all that I have said and a vast deal besides. But as things are, "for the days are evil," it is enough now that you have been admonished not to give yourself up altogether, nor at all times, to the active life, but to set apart some portion of your heart and of your time for consideration. But in saying this I have regard to the necessity laid upon you, not to the claims of righteousness; albeit there is no unrighteousness in yielding to necessity. For if the fitting were possible, reason unanswerably shows that piety, which is profitable for all things, should under all conceivable circumstances be distinctly preferred, and that it ought, either alone or above all else, to be studiously cultivated.

Do you ask what piety is? It is leaving time for consideration. You may perhaps tell me that herein I differ from him who defines piety as the worship of God. I do not really differ from him. If you well consider the point, you will find that I have expressed his meaning in my own words,

only partly, however, I admit. What is so essential to the
worship of God as the practice to which He exhorts in the
psalm, "Be still and see that I am God" (Ps 45:11)? This
certainly is the chief object of consideration. Is anything,
in all respects, so influential as consideration? Does it not
by a kindly anticipation create the divisions of the active
life itself, in a manner rehearsing and arranging beforehand
what has to be done? There must be consideration lest
haply affairs that, foreseen and premeditated, might turn
out well, may, if precipitated, be fraught with peril. I have
no doubt, if you will recall the incidents, you will find
that in law cases, important business of various kinds, or
in weighty deliberations, you have yourself frequently had
this sorrowful experience. First of all, consideration purifies
the very fountain, that is the mind, from which it springs.
Then it governs the affections, directs our actions, corrects
excesses, softens the manners, adorns and regulates the life,
and, lastly, bestows the knowledge of things divine and
human alike. It is consideration that brings order out of
disorder, puts in the links, pulls things together, investigates
mysteries, traces the truth, weighs probabilities, exposes
shams and counterfeits. It is consideration which arranges
beforehand what is to be done, and ponders what is accomplished, so that nothing faulty, or needing correction, may
settle in the mind. It is consideration which in prosperity
feels the sting of adversity, in adversity it is as though it felt
not; the one is fortitude, the other is prudence.[61]

---

[61] Saint Bernard, *On Consideration*, trans. George Lewis (Oxford:
Clarendon Press, 1908), bk. I, chaps. 5-7, pars. 22-27. In the
French edition of Bernard's treatise, the Latin word *consideratio* is

Meditation

Following Saint Bernard, let us learn to consider, to pray. Praying is, in the first place, looking attentively at Jesus. The Letter to the Hebrews defines and completes in a more detailed way what prayer is: "Therefore, holy brethren, who share in a heavenly call, consider Jesus, the apostle and high priest of our confession. He was faithful to him who appointed him, just as Moses also was faithful in God's house" (Heb 3:1-2). This is the same idea expressed in the Acts of the Apostles during the martyrdom of Saint Stephen: "But [Stephen], full of the Holy Spirit, gazed into heaven and saw the glory of God, and Jesus standing at the right hand of God.... And he knelt down and cried with a loud voice: 'Lord, do not hold this sin against them.' And when he had said this, he fell asleep" (Acts 7:55, 60).

All of us, but more specifically we priests, are invited to a life of contemplation. For,

> unless [the priest or] the missionary is a contemplative he cannot proclaim Christ in a credible way. He is a witness to the experience of God, and must be able to say with the apostles: "that which we have looked upon ... concerning the word of life,... we proclaim also to you." (1 Jn 1:1, 3)[62]

We are therefore exhorted to contemplate Christ in glory, seated at the right hand of the Father. Frequent, intense, and intimate prayer revives our filial relationship with God and makes us more

---

translated as *considération*, but the author systematically replaces it with "prayer." *Consideratio* can refer both to reflection on temporal matters and to mental prayer.

[62] John Paul II, Encyclical *Redemptoris missio* (December 7, 1990), no. 91.

aware of the vital necessity of our personal relations with Him. This contemplative prayer has a fundamental importance for priestly life; it is inexhaustibly fruitful and unfailingly efficacious. What can God refuse to a prayer that comes from a heart that loves and lives in the truth? True prayer, that silent and contemplative look at Jesus, strengthens faith. Tertullian confirms this in his treatise *On Prayer*. In it he writes:

> We are true worshipers and true priests. We pray in the Spirit, and so offer in the Spirit the sacrifice of prayer. Prayer is an offering that belongs to God and is acceptable to him: it is the offering he has asked for, the offering he planned as his own. We must dedicate this offering with our whole heart, we must fatten it on faith, tend it by truth, keep it unblemished through innocence and clean through chastity, and crown it with love. We must escort it to the altar of God in a procession of good works to the sound of psalms and hymns. Then it will gain for us all that we ask of God.[63]

The Risen Christ, Our Lord and Our God, is worthy of faith. We must adhere unreservedly to His Word, to His teaching, to His commandments, and to His laws; then our prayer will be heard and answered according to God's holy will.

The Letter to the Hebrews states that contemplating the glorified Christ produces another form of prayer, which we can call the prayer of attentive, silent listening. For praying is not only speaking to God, singing for the Lord, or reciting prayers, but

[63] Tertullian, *On Prayer*, in *The Liturgy of the Hours* (New York: Catholic Book Publishing, 1976), 2:249. Capitalization as in the French edition.

managing to keep silence so as to listen to the Holy Spirit. Saint Paul says, indeed, that

> we do not know how to pray as we ought, but the Spirit himself intercedes for us with sighs too deep for words. And he who searches the hearts of men knows what is the mind of the Spirit, because the Spirit intercedes for the saints according to the will of God. (Rom 8:26-27)

This is why the Letter to the Hebrews immediately combines the invitation to contemplate with an exhortation to listen. And so, quoting Psalm 95, it says: "O that today you would listen to his voice! Harden not your hearts" (Ps 95:7-8; cf. Heb 3:7-8, 15; 4:9). These words are repeated three times to underscore the importance of the prayer of listening. This listening mobilizes and engages our whole intellect, our will, our freedom, our whole heart, and our body. We see that Christian contemplation is not the passive attitude of a spectator. It requires and involves our whole being. Moreover, contemplating the glory of Christ drives us to be attentive to an interior call that sets us in motion toward God, produces in us an active docility, makes us more aware of our heavenly vocation (Heb 3:1), and encourages us to suppress our internal noise and the racket of the world and to prepare ourselves to enter into the Kingdom of God. This contemplation-listening is precisely what Peter, James, and John experienced on Mount Tabor during the Transfiguration of Jesus. There too, they were invited to pass from vision to hearing:

> [Jesus] was transfigured before them, and his face shone like the sun, and his garments became white as light.... He was still speaking, when ... a voice from the cloud said, "This is my beloved Son, with whom I am well pleased; listen to

him." When the disciples heard this, they fell on their faces, and were filled with awe. (Mt 17:2, 5-6)

For us priests, to pray is also to accept trials and sufferings. So many are entrusted to us in our ministry! This is why contemplative prayer requires us to contemplate often the Passion of Christ and His glory in Heaven so as to stimulate and encourage us to accept with faith, serenity, and love the persecutions, trials, and sufferings inherent in priestly life. When we practice contemplative prayer or pray, let us think of Jesus in the Garden of Gethsemane, who begs us: "My soul is very sorrowful, even to death; remain here, and watch with me" (Mt 26:38). Meditation on the sufferings that Jesus endured on behalf of sinners and the contemplation of His glory will surely be a source of energy to keep us from failing because of the weariness of our souls. Is this not what the Risen Jesus tried to make the disciples in Emmaus understand when they were disappointed, sad, and discouraged: "Was it not necessary that the Christ should suffer these things and enter into his glory?" (Lk 24:26).

Indeed, in faith we do not contemplate the glory of Jesus as a reality outside of us. Through faith, we are certain that we have already become "sharers in Christ" (see Heb 3:14), have already received "a kingdom that cannot be shaken" (Heb 12:28), and have already been admitted "to enter the sanctuary by the blood of Jesus, by the new and living way which he opened for us through the curtain, that is, through his flesh" (Heb 10:19-20).

We can also enter into contemplative prayer by taking as our guide this exhortation: "Let us draw near to God." This is an original and very priestly way of explaining what contemplative prayer is. Generally, the vocabulary of contemplation is static. The one who contemplates is in a state of quiet, of interior rest and serene tranquility. He feels that his faculties are calmed in a profound, living gaze in the presence of the divine majesty, and he stands before God with all the vigor of his intellect and the tenderness of his charity. Now the expression "to draw near to God," or "to approach God," or "to stand before God" (Gen 18:22–23; Deut 29:10; 1 Sam 6:20; 1 Kings 17:1), indicates a movement: to walk, enter, advance, and approach. The New Testament designates priests not by saying "those who contemplate Christ," or even "those who call on the name of the Lord." Rather, they are designated as those who, through Christ, draw near to God, since He is always alive to intercede on their behalf (see Heb 7:25). The most energetic exhortation in the Letter to the Hebrews is this: "Let us then with confidence draw near to the throne of grace, that we may receive mercy and find grace to help in time of need" (Heb 4:16). And because this is the most important exhortation in the whole letter, it is repeated: "Let us draw near with a true heart in full assurance of faith, with our hearts sprinkled clean from an evil conscience and our bodies washed with pure water" (Heb 10:22). This dynamic invitation to draw near to God goes beyond the simple exhortation to prayer. It influences the whole priestly life and existence. It aims at an ever more personal and intimate relationship with God, by virtue of Christ's sacrifice. The invitation to walk with confidence, in interior peace, is the specific feature of the priest's situation in its astounding novelty. It shows the primordial importance of prayer and of the liturgy, experienced in a setting of silent recollection, as an interior movement toward God.

Priestly life, like Christian life, is a liturgical way of life and therefore a permanent relationship with the Lord. We emphasize how distinctly privileged the situation of Christians appears in comparison with that of the Israelites, when we refer to their respective forms of worship. In the Old Testament, the organization of divine worship was regulated by numerous severe prohibitions. It was not permitted to approach God. The high priest himself was not authorized to enter the sanctuary freely to offer the prayers of the people to God. He could do this only once a year, during a solemn ceremony of expiation. For all the others, the prohibition was permanent, under pain of death (Lev 16:1-2). The great novelty proclaimed by the New Testament, and specifically by the Letter to the Hebrews, is that, thanks to Christ, entrance is free: Christians, and specifically, priests, have the *parrhesia*: the right and the freedom to appear before the Lord—not, of course, in liturgical vulgarity, disrespect, and trivialization, but with fear, awe, trembling, and a keen sense of the sacredness of this moment of contact with God. They will vigilantly be reconciled first with God and their neighbor, and they will prostrate themselves, like "the twenty-four elders [of the book of Revelation],... before Him who is seated on the Throne and worship Him who lives for ever and ever; and they will cast their crowns before the Throne of God" (see Rev 4:10).

This new situation obviously produces significant changes in the liturgy: from now on, Christ always has the absolute primacy in it. He is its center. He is the one who offers Himself anew on the Cross. He is the one who celebrates and associates us with His celebration so as to make us enter into the mystery of His Passion, death, and Resurrection. We priests are mere instruments, stewards of the mysteries of Christ. We are only the guardians and protectors of the deposit of faith, with the help of the Holy Spirit, Who dwells within us (see 2 Tim 1:13-14). Thus, the liturgy is no longer merely the external celebration of a ritual but, rather, the spiritual dynamism that springs from Christ's sacrifice. In the liturgy, everything starts from Christ and leads to Him. Everything is Christ's work, to which He associates His Church. It is therefore clear that the invitation to draw near to God through Christ first comes about in the Christian liturgy. When it is rightly understood and carried out correctly, the liturgy is far from being folklore, a display of our own cultural or ancestral heritage. It is *opus Dei*, a work of God for our salvation. Thus, in the Eucharistic liturgy, the greatest Christian prayer, we enter into the sanctuary thanks to the blood and the flesh of Christ and under the guidance of our High Priest: Christ. We go with Him to God, inspired by faith, hope, and charity. Our prayer as priests must enter into this great mystery of Christ's offering and sacrifice.

> But when Christ had offered for all time a single sacrifice for sins, he sat down at the right hand of God, then to wait until his enemies should be made a stool for his feet. For by a single offering he has perfected for all time those who are sanctified. (Heb 10:12-14)

The Letter to the Hebrews uses a dynamic formula. It says: "Through Him then let us continually offer up a sacrifice of praise to God, that is, the fruit of lips that acknowledge his name" (Heb 13:15). And to say "offer," the original text uses a verb that expresses an upward movement: "we lift up a sacrifice," as though to say that we are in the context of a Eucharistic celebration. The Eucharist is certainly the most significant and the most important moment in this sacrifice of praise, but the orientation that is received then should extend to the whole life of a priest. Our whole day and all our priestly activities must be a perpetual Eucharistic celebration, a perpetual prayer. We find again here a thought and several convictions dear to Saint Paul:

> Give thanks in all circumstances; for this is the will of God in Christ Jesus for you. (1 Thess 5:18)

> Addressing one another in psalms and hymns and spiritual songs, singing and making melody to the Lord with all your heart, always and for everything giving thanks in the name of our Lord Jesus Christ to God the Father. (Eph 5:19-20)

And whatever you do, in word or deed, do everything in the
name of the Lord Jesus, giving thanks to God the Father
through him. (Col 3:17)

The prayer of praise should imbue and involve our whole lives as
priests and be our perpetual offering.

Sacrifice is the most complete form of prayer, the most perfect
manner of entering into a close relationship with God. Christ showed
that sacrifice offered to God and devotion toward our brothers and
sisters are not two separate sectors of our life. His sacrifice on the Cross
united in the closest possible way the two dimensions of love, being at
the same time and primarily an act of perfect filial obedience to God
and the highest expression of love for human beings, His brethren.
Following Jesus' example and with the strength that we obtain in
His sacrifice, Christian and priestly life must continually unite these
two dimensions: the offering of prayer and the offering of charity.

Note that these two aspects are even less separable because we
do good for others by praying for them too. Praying for one another
is a very important form of genuine Christian charity (Heb 13:18).

Father Albert Vanhoye writes, "Not only is Christian prayer
illuminated by this mystery thanks to our contemplation of Christ,
but it is also conformed with and reliant on the present intervention of Christ, Who, acknowledging that we are His brothers,
opens up for us the possibility of going to God confidently and
imparts to our life a movement of generous offering."[64]

Like the Apostles, let us humbly say to Jesus: "Lord, teach us
to pray, as John taught his disciples" (Lk 11:1).

---

[64] Albert Vanhoye, *Le Don du Christ*, in the series "Lecture spirituelle"
(Paris: Bayard, 2005), 48.

VII

Concrete Sanctity

Based on a meditation by Benedict XVI

Introduction

I often get the impression that meetings, retreats, and synods recall great and beautiful truths but that all this changes nothing about everyday life. These great assemblies of bishops or priests are often content to write pretty reflections and to publish documents that are intellectually well constructed and careful to adapt themselves to the modern spirit and mentalities of Western societies. Very rarely are other peoples of the world taken into account. You get the impression that they would like to bring the whole world around to a purely Western vision of things, of mankind, and of history. Everything seems to be organized, thought out, and pastorally resolved solely according to the preoccupations and problems of the West, as though the Catholic Church were European only and nothing else. Sometimes this runs the risk of falsifying the Word of God (see 1 Cor 2:16; 2 Cor 4:2), of straying from Him who said: "I am the Way, the Truth, and the Life," and of betraying the revelation and the perennial teaching of the Church. Some documents or certain statements seem unconcerned with helping the Christian faithful to encounter Jesus Christ, to accept in their entirety the radical demands of His gospel, and to strengthen their faith, for the purpose of really conforming us to Him. We have a tendency to "spiritualize" (in the bad sense of the term) the Christian realities. We make ideas and phantoms out of them. For example, at the start of Lent, preachers often recall that the fast that matters is the fast of the heart and of the mind. They insist on saying that fasting is not primarily an external exercise, an ascetical exploit. All this is correct and good. But they insist on it so much that they end up neglecting the fasting of the body, which supports the fasting of the heart. We mistake ourselves for angels and think that recalling a truth is enough to put it into practice. We do need concrete means of achieving this. The example of Christ, who fasted for forty days and forty nights, invites us to do as He did. Moses fasted repeatedly for forty days and forty nights, every time he encountered God "to receive the tables of stone, the tables of the covenant which the LORD made with [us]" (Deut 9:9; cf. Exod 34:29). During the season of Lent, in which the ancient discipline underscores the importance of bodily self-control through fasting, abstinence, and night vigils, we are strongly urged to reflect on what the human body represents. The Gospel calls the body of Jesus a temple (Jn 2:13-25). The temple is the place where one offers sacrifices to God, the sacred space where God manifests Himself and where we can encounter Him face-to-face. On Good Friday, when the body of the Son of God was nailed to the Cross, a perfect, holy sacrifice pleasing to God was offered for the forgiveness of sins, and God revealed then how much He loved us, to the very end of love — in other words, unto death. For to love truly is to die for those whom one loves [see Jn 15:13]. How do we make our body participate concretely in the season of Lent?

How do we prepare it so that it might really be the temple of God? Why, then, have we stopped fasting concretely, corporeally? Why do we no longer agree to deprive ourselves of food, as Jesus did for forty days and forty nights? Do we find this penance and this mortification of our body excessive, useless, obsolete, and ill-suited to our era, in which production and consumption are signs of progress? Certainly, we must not be content to reduce our food intake. We must also and above all abstain absolutely from sin and combat our bad tendencies. It is very concretely incumbent on us to be renewed daily and to arm ourselves to battle "the old man that ... is corrupt through deceitful lusts, and be renewed in the spirit of [our] minds, and put on the new man, created after the likeness of God in true righteousness and holiness" (Eph 4:22-24). We must fight against the routine of our mortal condition. We all have to work so that no one remains in the vices of his former life.

Let us apply this to the priestly life. We must reread the Acts of the Apostles. After receiving the Holy Spirit on Pentecost, the Apostles, the first priests of the Church, were not content to praise God and to proclaim Him at the will of the Spirit's sober inebriation. They gave a Christocentric, ecclesial form and substance to their lives.

> The company of those who believed were of one heart and soul, and no one said that any of the things which he possessed was his own, but they had everything in common.... There was not any one needy among them, for as many as were possessors of lands or houses sold them, and brought the proceeds of what was sold and laid it at the apostles' feet; and distribution was made to each as any had need. (Acts 4:32, 34-35)

They held steadfastly to the apostles' teaching and fellowship, to the breaking of the bread and to the prayers. (Acts
2:42)

I dare to ask the question: what if we imitated the Apostles?
Wouldn't the form of apostolic life necessarily become the form of
priestly life? All the renewals in the history of the Church drew their
strength from a return to Pentecost. We need a priestly Pentecost.
We need the Holy Spirit in order to adopt the concrete means
of priestly holiness. Now, to be holy is to live out the theological
virtues perfectly and to behave as sons of God, exactly as our
Heavenly Father foresaw that we should behave. To be holy is to
conform ourselves to what God has destined for us and to strive
for it constantly—namely, to become sharers in the divine nature
(see 2 Pet 1:4). As long as we have not attained what we were made
for, we will experience within us an anxious restlessness of the soul,
which has a nostalgic desire for God. Saint Augustine expressed
this in a famous aphorism at the beginning of his *Confessions*: "You
made us for Yourself, Lord, and our hearts are restless until they
rest in You."[65] Because He, our God, is holy, we, too, must become
holy. The Lord addressed these words to Moses: "Say to all the
congregation of the sons of Israel, You shall be holy; for I the LORD
your God am holy" (Lev 19:2). God grants us to be holy, like Him,
because He is holy. We may think that this is an unattainable,
exorbitant, impossible ideal. Well then, if you feel demoralized
when, perhaps in an expecially acute way, you put your finger on
your littleness, the enormity of your sins, and the nothingness and
dust that you are, then place yourself with complete confidence in
God's hands, "for with God nothing will be impossible" (Lk 1:37).

[65] Augustine, *Confessions*, I, 1, 1.

He is capable of accomplishing in us what we were chosen to do before the beginning of the world. By ourselves and counting on our own abilities we are incapable of becoming holy. This is why Jesus prays to His Father, saying: "Sanctify them in the truth; your word is truth. . . . For their sake I consecrate myself, that they also may be consecrated in truth" (Jn 17:17, 19).

The story goes that one day a beggar happened to meet Alexander the Great and asked him for an alms. Alexander stopped and commanded that the beggar be made the ruler of five towns. The poor man, embarrassed and stunned, exclaimed, "I was not asking for so much!" And Alexander replied: "You asked according to what you are, but I give to you according to what I am." God always gives in a surprising way. God has already given everything to us as priests, according to what He is, through Jesus Christ. "No longer do I call you servants, for the servant does not know what his master is doing; but I have called you friends, for all that I have heard from my Father I have made known to you" (Jn 15:15).

Meeting of the Holy Father Benedict XVI with the clergy of the Diocese of Bolzano-Bressanone, August 6, 2008

I find myself together with all of you in the midst of this process of toil and interior struggle; I shall try to say a few words, precisely as part of a broader dialogue.

In my answer I would like to examine two fundamental aspects: on the one hand, the irreplaceableness of the priest, the meaning and the manner of the priestly ministry today; and on the other—and this is more obvious than it used to be—the multiplicity of charisms and the fact that all together they are Church, they build the Church and for this reason we must strive to reawaken charisms. Together we must foster this living institution, so that it might then support the priest. He supports others, others support him, and only in this complex and variegated whole can the Church grow today and advance toward the future.

On the one hand, there will always be a need for the priest who is totally dedicated to the Lord and therefore totally dedicated to humanity. In the Old Testament there is the call to "sanctification" which more or less corresponds to what we mean today by "consecration," or even "priestly Ordination": something is delivered over to God and is therefore removed from the common sphere; it is given to Him. Yet this means that it is now available for all. Since it has been taken away and given to God, for this very reason it is now not isolated but has been lifted up into "pro-existence," into being "for all." I think that this can also be said of the Church's priesthood. It means on the one hand that we are entrusted to the Lord, withdrawn from ordinary life, but on the other, we are entrusted to Him so that in this way we can belong to Him totally and totally belong to others. I believe that we must continuously seek to show this to young people—to those who are idealists, who want to do something for humanity as a whole—show them that precisely this "removal from the common sphere" means "gift to the whole" and that this is an important way, the most important way, to serve our brethren. Another part of this is truly making oneself available to the Lord in the totality of one's being and, consequently, finding oneself totally available to men and women. I think that celibacy is a fundamental expression of this totality and already, for this reason, an important reminder in this world, because it has meaning only if we truly believe in eternal life and if we believe that God involves us and that we can respond to His call.

Therefore, the priesthood is indispensable because in the Eucharist itself, originating in God, it constantly builds up the Church; in the Sacrament of Penance it constantly confers purification on us; in the Sacrament, the priesthood is, precisely, an involvement in the "for" [pro-existence] of Jesus Christ. However, I know very well how difficult it is today—when a priest finds himself directing not only one easily managed parish but several parishes and pastoral units; when he must be available to give this or that advice, and so forth—how difficult it is to live such a life. I think that in this situation it is important to have the courage to limit oneself and to be clear about deciding on priorities. One fundamental priority of priestly life is to be with the Lord and thus to have time for prayer. Saint Charles Borromeo always used to say: "You will not be able to care for the souls of others if you let your own perish. In the end you will no longer do anything even for others. You must always have time for yourself to be with God." I would therefore like to emphasize this: whatever demands may arise, it is a real priority to find every day, I would say, an hour to be in silence for the Lord and with the Lord, as the Church suggests we do with the breviary, with daily prayers, so that we can be enriched interiorly again and again, so as to be centered again—as I said in answering the first question—within the reach of the Holy Spirit's breath. And to order priorities on this basis: I must learn to see what is truly essential, where my presence as a priest is indispensable and I cannot delegate someone else. And at the same time, I must humbly accept the fact that when there are many things I should do and where my presence is requested, I cannot manage it because I know my limits. I think that people will understand this humility.

And I now must link this to the other aspect: knowing how to delegate, to get people to collaborate. I have the impression that people understand and also appreciate it when a priest is with God, when he is concerned with his responsibility of being the person who prays for others: they say, "We cannot pray that much, you must do it for us: basically, it is your job, as it were, to be the one who prays for us." They want a priest who honestly endeavours to live with the Lord and then is available to men and women—the suffering, the dying, the sick, children, young people (I would say that these are the priorities)—but also who can discern the things that others can do better than he can, thereby making room for those gifts. I am thinking of Movements and of many other forms of collaboration in the parish. Everyone in a diocese reflects together on all this too; they create forms of collaboration and encourage exchanges. You rightly said that in this it is important to look beyond the parish to the diocesan community, indeed, to the community of the universal Church, which in turn must look at what is happening in the parish and what the consequences are for the individual priest.

You then touched on another point that is very important in my view: even if priests live far apart, they are a true community of brothers who should support and help one another. Today more than ever this communion among priests is important. In order not to drift into isolation, into loneliness with its sorrows, it is important for us to meet one another regularly. It will be the task of the diocese to establish how best to organize meetings for priests—today we have cars which make travelling easier—so that we can experience being together ever anew, learn from one another, mutually correct and help one another, encourage and comfort one another, so that in this communion of the presbyterate, together with our Bishop, we can carry out our service to the local Church. No priest is a priest on his own; we are a presbyterate and only in this communion with the Bishop can each one offer his service. Now, this beautiful communion, which is acknowledged by all at the theological level, must also be expressed in practice in a way identified by the local Church. And it must be extended, because no bishop is a bishop on his own but only a bishop in the College, in the great communion of bishops. This is the communion we should always strive for. And I think that it is a particularly beautiful aspect of Catholicism: through the Primacy, which is not an absolute monarchy but a service of communion, we can have the certainty of this unity. Thus in a large community with many voices, all together we make the great music of faith ring out in this world.

Let us pray the Lord to comfort us whenever we think we cannot manage any longer: let us support one another, and only then will the Lord help us to find the right paths together.[66]

[66] English translation at the Vatican website, slightly emended.

For Eternity

---<∞>---

Meditation

We must therefore unite with Christ through faith, allow His life to penetrate to our innermost depths and be manifested there. Holiness gives us membership in an immense crowd of authentic disciples of Christ; these form the Church, His Body: a Mystical Body made up of various races of men and women, the young and the old, the poor and the rich, sinners and saints. Every Sunday, when Christian believers meet for adoration, they become a temple in which Jesus Christ renews His purifying and sanctifying sacrifice and in which God is present. At the heart of the Eucharistic celebration, which is experienced in faith, recollection, silence, and reverential fear, look at those who are gathered there by the breath of the Spirit: you know immediately that you see the Body of Christ. Look at God, and you will see their faces—whether tired or radiant with an interior joy—their discreet smiles or their tears, and you will know that you see there the face of Christ. They are the Body that Jesus promised to raise from the dead. This is precisely the reason the Acts of the Apostles asks us the question about common life. The book calls to us. For us priests, is it normal, is it humanly and spiritually edifying, to live alone? However majestic a river may be, it needs a source and tributaries in order to swell its waters; otherwise, it dwindles and dries up. Is it normal, is it desirable, to pray each day, alone, the hours of the Divine Office? Shouldn't this situation be painful for us, at least? Do we not have to hope to give the witness of fraternal, common life?

I have no miraculous solution to propose to you. But I am sure of one thing: our witness is not credible if we are incapable of a life of concrete charity and therefore of a life in common. "The fruit of the Spirit is love, joy, peace, patience, kindness, goodness, faithfulness, gentleness, self-control" (Gal 5:22–23). The fruit of each Eucharist is this unity among us, this common life and Christian fraternity that makes us brothers and sisters, because the blood of Christ flows in our veins. The breviary is designed to be prayed and chanted in common and experienced in community. What if we dared to make that possible?

I think that the people of God need to observe and experience the fact that priests are the first ones to live like the Apostles. The faithful want to see their priests pray together and live together in charity. What credibility will sacramental communion have if it is not lived out in fraternal communion?

There is an urgent mission for the bishops here. It is up to them to offer priests the emotional and realistic conditions for common life. This is not just an aid for their individual personal life. Common life is part of the identity of the priesthood:

All priests, who are constituted in the order of priesthood by the sacrament of Orders, are bound together by an intimate sacramental brotherhood; but in a special way they form one priestly body (*presbyterium*) in the diocese to which they are attached under their own bishop. For even though they may be assigned different duties, yet they fulfill the one priestly service for the people.... For this reason it is of great importance that all priests, whether diocesan or regular, should help each other, so that they may be fellow-helpers of the truth. Each is joined to the rest of the members of this priestly body (*presbyterium*) by special ties of apostolic charity, of ministry, and of brotherhood.... So priests are all united with their brother-priests by the bond of charity, prayer, and total cooperation.[67]

[67] Vatican Council II, Decree on the Ministry and Life of Priests *Presbyterorum ordinis* (December 7, 1965), no. 8.

For Eternity

A solitary life cannot manifest the fullness of the mystery of Christ the Priest. And as the Acts of the Apostles reminds us, common life, liturgical prayer in common, the sharing of goods in charity is the first fruit of the Holy Spirit. If we do not see this fruit, then we can doubt the presence of the Spirit. Let us dare to ask ourselves concrete questions. I think that the first place in which this common life of prayer, charity, and apostolate should be experienced is the Roman Curia. Presently the holy life of many priests there is obscured by the scandals and ambitions of a few. I dare to dream: What if we in the Curia took the Acts of the Apostles seriously? Would it be impossible for the cardinals to live around the pope, to pray together, to share a sober, common table? Maybe this is the reform of the Curia that would be the most evangelical! Pope Francis lets us experience this during the days of the annual spiritual exercises, during which we share together the same Eucharist, the same meals, the same moments of listening to the Word of God in meditation and prayer, in a godly atmosphere of recollection, silence, and solitude. Could we not experience it concretely throughout the year? What a joy it would be to share concretely our happiness in being priests! Certainly, common life is not always easy. It is demanding. But it is enough to visit monastic communities to know that it is the source of a profound, infectious joy.

VIII

The Radical Character of the Gospel

Based on a meditation by Saint John Paul II

Introduction

The Second Vatican Council gave us a deeper understanding of specifically priestly holiness. During the 1990 synod, the whole Church assimilated Her teaching so as to call priests more persuasively to a radical way of life according to the Gospel. Very often we tend to think that the evangelical counsels—poverty, chastity, and obedience—are reserved for consecrated religious. They are offered to all baptized persons, however, and, in a specific way, to priests. Unfortunately, priestly poverty and priestly obedience often remain very ethereal realities, academic speeches made by middle-class men seated on the chair of Moses (see Mt 23:2-5). We talk about it, we praise it, but do we put it into practice?

For all Christians, without exception, the radicalism of the gospel is a fundamental, irreplaceable requirement, a logical consequence of Christ's call to follow Him and imitate Him. All are called to holiness, but priests are called to it in a particular way. They must be holy specifically as priests. Since they are configured to Christ in a specific way, they must imitate Him in a particularly

For Eternity

radical way of living out the gospel. Many virtues are decisive for
the pastoral and spiritual life of a priest; for example, faith, humility with regard to the mystery of God, mercy, prudence. But the
"evangelical counsels" that Jesus teaches in the Sermon on the
Mount are the privileged expression of the radicalism of the gospel
(see Mt 5–7). Among these counsels, which are closely coordinated
with one another, are obedience, chastity, and poverty. "The priest
is called to live these counsels in accordance with those ways and,
more specifically, those goals and that basic meaning which derive
from and express his own priestly identity," says Saint John Paul II.[68]

Holiness seems an intrinsic requirement of the priesthood.
Father Albert Vanhoye writes:

> Before Christ, certainly, there was great concern for the
> holiness of priests, but only an external holiness could be
> provided: minutely prescribed rituals (ablutions, anoint-
> ings, special vestments) separated the priest materially from
> the profane world and symbolically consecrated him to
> God. This expressed the concern to make oneself worthy
> of God. But what can ceremonies or sacred garments do,
> if man's heart remains sullied? In his innermost depths the
> priest must be dedicated to God. Otherwise he could not
> be pleasing and acceptable.

This radical requirement finds its complete fulfillment in Jesus
Christ, and in Him alone. Christ's holiness is not like a ceremonial vestment, designed to mask the priest's personal unworthiness. It is an interior holiness, which springs up in him as the
very source of his being, fills him entirely, and spreads with an
impetuous force.

---

[68] *Pastores dabo vobis* 27.

---◆∞◆---

Saint John Paul II, *Pastores dabo vobis*: Priestly Life and the Radicalism of the Gospel

For all Christians without exception, the radicalism of the Gospel represents a fundamental, undeniable demand flowing from the call of Christ to follow and imitate him by virtue of the intimate communion of life with him brought about by the Spirit (cf. Mt 8:18-20; 10:37-39; Mk 8:34-38; 10:17-21; Lk 9:57-62). This same demand is made anew to priests, not only because they are "in" the Church, but because they are "in the forefront" of the Church inasmuch as they are configured to Christ, the Head and Shepherd, equipped for and committed to the ordained ministry, and inspired by pastoral charity. Within and as a manifestation of the radicalism of the Gospel one can find a blossoming of many virtues and ethical demands which are decisive for the pastoral and spiritual life of the priest, such as faith, humility in relation to the mystery of God, mercy and prudence. A particularly significant expression of the radicalism of the Gospel is seen in the different "evangelical counsels" which Jesus proposes in the Sermon on the Mount (cf. Mt 5-7), and among them the intimately related counsels of obedience, chastity and poverty. The priest is called to live these counsels in accordance with those ways and, more specifically, those goals and that basic meaning which derive from and express his own priestly identity.

"Among the virtues most necessary for the priestly ministry must be named that disposition of soul by which priests are always ready to seek not their own will, but the will of him who sent them (cf. Jn 4:34; 5:30; 6:38)."[69] It is in the spiritual life of the priest that obedience takes on certain special characteristics.

First of all, obedience is "apostolic" in the sense that it recognizes, loves, and serves the Church in her hierarchical structure. Indeed, there can be no genuine priestly ministry except in communion with the Supreme Pontiff and the episcopal college, especially with one's own diocesan bishop, who deserves that "filial respect and obedience" promised during the rite of ordination. This "submission" to those invested with ecclesial authority is in no way a kind of humiliation. It flows instead from the responsible freedom of the priest who accepts not only the demands of an organized and organic ecclesial life, but also that grace of discernment and responsibility in ecclesial decisions which was assured by Jesus to his apostles and their successors for the sake of faithfully safeguarding the mystery of the Church and serving the structure of the Christian community among its common path toward salvation.

Authentic Christian obedience, when it is properly motivated and lived without servility, helps the priest to exercise in accordance with the Gospel the authority entrusted to him for his work with the People of God: an authority free from authoritarianism or demagoguery. Only the person who knows how to obey in Christ is really able to require obedience from others in accordance with the Gospel.

Priestly obedience has also a "community" dimension: It is not the obedience of an individual who alone relates

---

[69] Vatican Council II, *Presbyterorum ordinis* 15.

to authority, but rather an obedience which is deeply a part of the unity of the presbyterate, which as such is called to cooperate harmoniously with the bishop and, through him, with Peter's successor.[70]

This aspect of the priest's obedience demands a marked spirit of asceticism, both in the sense of a tendency not to become too bound up in one's own preferences or points of view and in the sense of giving brother priests the opportunity to make good use of their talents, and abilities, setting aside all forms of jealousy, envy, and rivalry. Priestly obedience should be one of solidarity, based on belonging to a single presbyterate. Within the presbyterate, this obedience is expressed in co-responsibility regarding directions to be taken and choices to be made.

Finally, priestly obedience has a particular "pastoral" character. It is lived in an atmosphere of constant readiness to allow oneself to be taken up, as it were "consumed," by the needs and demands of the flock. These last ought to be truly reasonable and at times they need to be evaluated and tested to see how genuine they are. But it is undeniable that the priest's life is fully "taken up" by the hunger for the Gospel and for faith, hope, and love for God and his mystery, a hunger which is more or less consciously present in the People of God entrusted to him.

Referring to the evangelical counsels, the Council states that "preeminent among these counsels is that precious gift of divine grace given to some by the Father (cf. Mt 19:11; 1 Cor 7:7) in order more easily to devote themselves to God alone with an undivided heart (cf. 1 Cor 7:32–34) in

[70] See *Presbyterorum ordinis* 15.

virginity or celibacy. This perfect continence for love of the kingdom of heaven has always been held in high esteem by the Church as a sign and stimulus of love, and as a singular source of spiritual fertility in the world."[71] In virginity and celibacy, chastity retains its original meaning, that is, of human sexuality lived as a genuine sign of and precious service to the love of communion and gift of self to others. This meaning is fully found in virginity which makes evident, even in the renunciation of marriage, the "nuptial meaning" of the body through a communion and a personal gift to Jesus Christ and his Church which prefigures and anticipates the perfect and final communion and self-giving of the world to come: "In virginity or celibacy, the human being is awaiting, also in a bodily way, the eschatological marriage of Christ with the Church, giving himself or herself completely to the Church in the hope that Christ may give himself to the Church in the full truth of eternal life."[72]

In this light one can more easily understand and appreciate the reasons behind the centuries-old choice which the Western Church has made and maintained — despite all the difficulties and objections raised down the centuries — of conferring the order of presbyter only on men who have given proof that they have been called by God to the gift of chastity in absolute and perpetual celibacy.

The Synod Fathers clearly and forcefully expressed their thought on this matter in an important proposal which deserves to be quoted here in full:

[71] Lumen gentium 42.
[72] John Paul II, Apostolic Exhortation Familiaris consortio (November 22, 1981), no. 16; AAS 74 (1982): 98.

While in no way interfering with the discipline of the Oriental Churches, the Synod, in the conviction that perfect chastity in priestly celibacy is a charism, reminds priests that celibacy is a priceless gift of God for the Church and has a prophetic value for the world today. This Synod strongly reaffirms what the Latin Church and some Oriental rites require, that is, that the priesthood be conferred only on those men who have received from God the gift of the vocation to celibate chastity (without prejudice to the tradition of some Oriental Churches and particular cases of married clergy who convert to Catholicism, which are admitted as exceptions in Pope Paul VI's Encyclical on priestly celibacy, no. 42). The Synod does not wish to leave any doubts in the mind of anyone regarding the Church's firm will to maintain the law that demands perpetual and freely chosen celibacy for present and future candidates for priestly ordination in the Latin rite. The Synod would like to see celibacy presented and explained in the fullness of its biblical, theological, and spiritual richness, as a precious gift given by God to his Church and as a sign of the kingdom which is not of this world—a sign of God's love for this world and of the undivided love of the priest for God and for God's people, with the result that celibacy is seen as a positive enrichment of the priesthood.[73]

---

[73] *Propositio* 11.

It is especially important that the priest understand the theological motivation of the Church's law on celibacy. Inasmuch as it is a law, it expresses the Church's will, even before the will of the subject expressed by his readiness. But the will of the Church finds its ultimate motivation in the link between celibacy and sacred ordination, which configures the priest to Jesus Christ the Head and Spouse of the Church. The Church, as the Spouse of Jesus Christ, wishes to be loved by the priest in the total and exclusive manner in which Jesus Christ her Head and Spouse loved her. Priestly celibacy, then, is the gift of self in and with Christ to his Church and expresses the priest's service to the Church in and with the Lord.

For an adequate priestly spiritual life, celibacy ought not to be considered and lived as an isolated or purely negative element, but as one aspect of the positive, specific, and characteristic approach to being a priest. Leaving father and mother, the priest follows Jesus the Good Shepherd in an apostolic communion, in the service of the People of God. Celibacy, then, is to be welcomed and continually renewed with a free and loving decision as a priceless gift from God, as an "incentive to pastoral charity,"[74] as a singular sharing in God's fatherhood and in the fruitfulness of the Church, and as a witness to the world of the eschatological kingdom. To put into practice all the moral, pastoral and spiritual demands of priestly celibacy it is absolutely necessary that the priest pray humbly and trustingly, as the Council points out: "In the world today, many people call perfect continence impossible. The more they do so, the more humbly

[74] *Presbyterorum ordinis* 16.

and perseveringly priests should join with the Church in praying for the grace of fidelity. It is never denied to those who ask. At the same time let priests make use of all the supernatural and natural helps which are now available to all." Once again it is prayer, together with the Church's sacraments and ascetical practice, which will provide hope in difficulties, forgiveness in failings, and confidence and courage in resuming the journey.

On the subject of evangelical poverty, the Synod Fathers gave a concise yet important description, presenting it as "the subjection of all goods to the supreme good of God and his kingdom."[75] In reality, only the person who contemplates and lives the mystery of God as the one and supreme good, as the true and definitive treasure, can understand and practice poverty, which is certainly not a matter of despising or rejecting material goods but of a loving and responsible use of these goods and at the same time an ability to renounce them with great interior freedom—that is, with reference to God and his plan.

Poverty for the priest, by virtue of his sacramental configuration to Christ, the Head and Shepherd, takes on specific "pastoral" connotations which the Synod Fathers took up from the Council's teachings and further developed.[76] Among other things, they wrote: "Priests, following the example of Christ, who, rich though he was, became poor for love of us (cf. 2 Cor 8:9), should consider the poor and the weakest as people entrusted in a special way to them, and they should be capable of witnessing to poverty with

[75] *Propositio* 8.
[76] See *Presbyterorum ordinis* 17.

a simple and austere lifestyle, having learned the generous renunciation of superfluous things (*Optatam totius*, 9; *Code of Canon Law*, canon 282)."[77]

It is true that "the workman deserves his wages" (Lk 10:7) and that "the Lord commanded that those who proclaim the Gospel should get their living by the Gospel" (1 Cor 9:14), but it is no less true that this right of the apostle can in no way be confused with attempts of any kind to condition service to the Gospel and the Church upon the advantages and interests which can derive from it. Poverty alone ensures that the priest remains available to be sent wherever his work will be most useful and needed even at the cost of personal sacrifice. It is a condition and essential premise of the apostle's docility to the Spirit, making him ready to "go forth," without traveling bag or personalities, following only the will of the Master (cf. Lk 9:57-62; Mk 10:17-22).

Being personally involved in the life of the community and being responsible for it, the priest should also offer the witness of a total "honesty" in the administration of the goods of the community, which he will never treat as if they were his own property, but rather something for which he will be held accountable by God and his brothers and sisters, especially the poor. Moreover, his awareness of belonging to the one presbyterate will be an incentive for the priest to commit himself to promoting both a more equitable distribution of goods among his fellow priests and a certain common use of goods (cf. Acts 2:42-47).

[77] *Propositio* 10.

The interior freedom which is safeguarded and nourished by evangelical poverty will help the priest to stand beside the underprivileged; to practice solidarity with their efforts to create a more just society; to be more sensitive and capable of understanding and discerning realities involving the economic and social aspects of life; and to promote a preferential option for the poor. The latter, while excluding no one from the proclamation and gift of salvation, will assist him in gently approaching the poor, sinners, and all those on the margins of society, following the model given by Jesus in carrying out his prophetic and priestly ministry (cf. Lk 4:18).

Nor should the prophetic significance of priestly poverty be forgotten, so urgently needed in affluent and consumeristic societies: "A truly poor priest is indeed a specific sign of separation from, disavowal of and non-submission to the tyranny of a contemporary world which puts all its trust in money and in material security."[78]

Jesus Christ, who brought his pastoral charity to perfection on the cross with a complete exterior and interior emptying of self, is both the model and source of the virtues of obedience, chastity, and poverty which the priest is called to live out as an expression of his pastoral charity for his brothers and sisters. In accordance with St. Paul's words to the Christians at Philippi, the priest should have "the mind which was in Christ Jesus," emptying himself of his own "self," so as to discover, in a charity which is obedient, chaste, and poor, the royal road of union with God and unity with his brothers and sisters (cf. Phil 2:5).[79]

---

[78] *Propositio* 10.
[79] *Pastores dabo vobis* 27–30.

Meditation

How can we avoid indifference about the tragedy of sexual abuse and cases of the abuse of authority? I am convinced that they are rooted in the secularization of the life of priests. The priest is a man set apart for the service of God and of the Church. He is a consecrated man. His whole life is set aside for God. Now, some have tried to desacralize priestly life. They have tried to trivialize it, secularize it, and make it profane.

Priests have been formed without being taught that the only support of their lives is God, without having experienced the fact that their lives have meaning only by God and for Him. Deprived of God, nothing remained for them except human power. Some have sunk into the diabolical logic of abuse of authority and sexual crimes. Unless a priest experiences every day the fact that he is only an instrument in God's hands, unless he stands constantly before God to serve Him with all his heart, then he runs the risk of being inebriated by a sense of power. If the life of a priest is not a consecrated life, then he is in great danger of being deluded and going astray.

Now, celibacy demonstrates most obviously that the priest belongs to Christ and that he no longer belongs to himself. Celibacy is the sign of a life that has meaning only through God and for Him.

With respect to the married Eastern-rite clergy, I would like to emphasize several points. The profound being of a priest consists of an identification, a conformation to Christ, the Bridegroom of the Church. This reality is perfectly expressed and manifested by the state of celibate priests, whether in the East or the West. Indeed, we must not overlook the fact that many diocesan priests of the Eastern Catholic Churches chose to live as celibates. Pope Saint John Paul II, that great friend of the Christian East, had taught us this very clearly in the Apostolic Exhortation *Pastores dabo vobis*: "And so priestly celibacy should not be considered just as a legal norm or as a totally external condition for admission to ordination, but rather as a value that is profoundly connected with ordination, whereby a man takes on the likeness of Jesus Christ, the Good Shepherd and Spouse of the Church."[80]

Of course, every priest lives by this mystery, at least interiorly. But this is less evident and manifest for the Church and the People of God in the case of married priests. In no way do I call into question the personal holiness of each one of them. I know the extent to which they devote themselves every day to the Church of God. If I could meet them personally, I would kiss their hands, which have been consecrated by the holy oil, hands that every day touch the precious Body of Jesus Christ, hands that give absolution and bless. But I must say that celibate priests give a sign that is necessary for the whole Church so that She understands that She is the Bride of Christ.

I would like to cite at some length a great theologian and very subtle expert on ancient Tradition, Father Louis Bouyer:

> The Church in the West requires of all her priests not only chastity, but celibacy. In the East the requirement of it is not as strict, but the ideal that it holds up for the clergy is still more explicit, despite everything. Eastern-rite priests cannot contract marriage after their consecration, any more than those of the Latin rite can. If they were married before being ordained to the priesthood, they are merely permitted to persevere in the married state.
>
> However the Church, even in the East, is quite definite about the point that consecration to the priestly ministry

---

[80] *Pastores dabo vobis* 50.

requires, at least as an ideal, the abandonment of everything for Christ: of the Bishop at least, in whom the Priesthood is present in its fullness and so to speak in its visible source, it requires not only that he practice celibacy but that he be totally devoted to Christ, before his consecration, through monastic profession. And it is clear for the priests of the second degree themselves, the state of life that the Church recommends without imposing it on them all is the state of the hieromonk: in other words, the state of a man whom complete monastic life, with all its requirements for detachment, has prepared for spiritual fatherhood, sealed by the priesthood....

Here the practice of the Eastern Church is especially illuminating. It shows us, indeed, that merely bodily chastity is by no means the one and only form of priestly self-denial and, consequently, that here it is not just a matter of the flesh, nor, *a fortiori*, of an exaggeratedly pessimistic view of it. Indeed, in making the priest-monk its ideal, the Eastern Church shows us that the chastity of a priest must be connected with a much more general spirit of poverty. In the chaste life that is required of him, the priest must master and surpass not only what is carnal, but all particular attachments, even to the best human realities.[81]

The priest's obedience is not professional submission to a hierarchical superior. It comes within the scope of the Son's obedience to the Father; it participates in it and prolongs it.

[81] Louis Bouyer, *Le sens de la vie sacerdotale* (Paris: Éditions du Cerf, 2008), chap. 7.

Like Christ, the priest must be able to declare: "My teaching is not mine, but his who sent me" (Jn 7:16). "For I have not spoken on my own authority; the Father who sent me has himself given me commandment what to say and what to speak" (Jn 12:49). And I must obey Him absolutely, unto death, even death on the Cross (see Phil 2:8).

A priest does not speak about himself, about his experience. He is sent to announce a message of which he is not the author. His fidelity to the Word of God, as handed down by the Church, is the root of his obedience. We do not expect a priest to be original, but rather faithful to the doctrine that has been transmitted.

So it is regrettable that some people, concerned about pleasing the world or wanting to seem up to date, but sometimes also to hide or reduce the radical requirements of the Word of God, have a tendency nowadays to dilute the gospel, to falsify it or to sugarcoat it so as to adapt it to Western mentalities and ideologies. Saint Paul already deplored this in his day when he wrote to the Corinthians: "For we are not, like so many, peddlers of God's word; but as men of sincerity, as commissioned by God, in the sight of God we speak in Christ" (2 Cor 2:17). Today there is a lot of ambiguity, confusion, and ideological interpretation of the Word of Jesus. An unprecedented level of relativism has been reached, even in the Church. This crucifies Christ again and ruins the gospel message. Nevertheless, Jesus left no doubt whatsoever about the radical character of His message and of His demands. For He, Jesus, is the Way, the Truth, and the Life: "Jesus Christ is the same yesterday and today and for ever" (Heb 13:8). What He required then, He requires just as much today. His gospel does not change at the world's tempo. On the contrary, it becomes more radical, the more it leads us toward the perfect accomplishment of the work of salvation, toward the creation of "the new man, created after the likeness of God in true righteousness and holiness" (Eph 4:24).

Since the origins of Christianity, inescapable choices have come to light: "No one can serve two masters; for either he will hate the one and love the other, or he will be devoted to the one and despise the other. You cannot serve God and mammon" (Mt 6:24; Lk 16:13). Either we follow Jesus, or we choose to conform to the world.

Church history is marked, as though with milestones, by the testimonies of a multitude of Christians who preferred to say no, even if it cost them their lives, rather than to lose the treasure that they had discovered in Jesus (Mt 13:44). Again in our present century, this sovereign freedom that faith in Jesus Christ gives has led Christians to resist victoriously the new ideologies that demolish the human being, the family, and our societies.

Many people in our time become irritated as soon as anyone speaks about truth and refers to a universal, objective truth that is outside of us, beyond us, and imperative for us. To them, that seems like a synonym for dogmatism, fundamentalism, and intolerance, as though it were contrary to science. They refuse to acknowledge the supreme reality of God. Nevertheless, the Word of God is the only light that reveals the truth about the world. People also insist a lot on cultural change nowadays. They speak about a new global ethics and paradigm shifts. Should the doctrinal and moral teaching and the disciplines of the Church change too? Although there are things that change, there are also others that remain stable. Progress is made by the technological tools. But human beings remain the same. Our contemporaries live in a new context. Some enjoy new conveniences, while others experience new difficulties in life. But in mankind today, there is the same collection of goodness, fraternal solidarity, generosity, and aspirations to freedom and happiness, and the same collection of malice, perversion, greed, nastiness, brutality, concupiscence, and tendencies to idolatry, as there was in mankind a thousand years ago: so deeply and ontologically marked are we by Original Sin. I am absolutely similar to Adam and Eve. The only difference between Adam and me is that I, today, have a mobile phone and a car. But this difference is superficial. In the deepest part of ourselves we have the same vices, the same ambitions, the same lusts, the same kinds of greed. And every human being who is born is obliged in turn to start over the efforts on behalf of moral and spiritual order that had been made by his parents or his grandparents. Everything has to be started over continually. This is the truth and the reality to which we owe obedience.

How tempting it is sometimes to say what the world would like to hear! How tempting it is to sugarcoat the Word of God, which is too strong for our dull minds! And yet, our obedience to its demands is the proof of our love for souls. What kind of Christians would we be if we taught them an adapted, easier doctrine? We would be forgers. We would lead souls by paths that lead nowhere. Our obedience guarantees our love to the very end.

And what should we say about poverty? People talk about it so much and practice it so little! How painful it is to observe that, in many regions of the world, priests behave like prominent citizens, like comfortable, middle-class persons. They display the exterior signs of wealth: a lot of money, travels, yearly vacations, automobile, house, computer. Certainly, material goods can and should be useful in proclaiming the kingdom of God. But if a priest is another Christ, then he is a poor man! There is nothing to discuss.

"Foxes have holes, and birds of the air have nests; but the Son of man has nowhere to lay his head" (Mt 8:20; Lk 9:58). It is difficult for a priest who lacks nothing, who has every comfort, all the earthly assurances of a tranquil life, to claim to imitate Jesus, to represent Him, and to be an extension of Him on this earth. How could he configure or conform himself to Jesus Christ and identify with Him? Poverty is essential to Christianity. It is a gospel value. Now, there are Catholic organizations whose purpose is to eradicate poverty and who have the senseless slogan "Zero poverty." But to eradicate poverty is to eradicate the gospel and the evangelical counsels. Certainly we must work relentlessly to eradicate misery, the extreme destitution caused by human greed and selfishness. But let us not forget the first Beatitude: "Blessed are the poor in spirit, for theirs is the kingdom of heaven" (Mt 5:3).

How constantly bishops and priests must improve their vigilance, wisdom, and prudence by letting themselves be taught and instructed by Jesus Christ!

The main challenge facing us is not our economic and social problems. Rather, the God of the Patriarchs, of the Prophets, and of Jesus Christ is the one who challenges us and confronts us with radical questions about the value and meaning of our life. As long as we allow ourselves to be questioned by men only, we come to a standstill, walk in circles, and give the impression that we no longer have any certitudes. God comes to lift us onto another level, that of Transcendence. He cannot make risky and possibly deceptive proposals. If we put the Beatitudes of the Gospel down on the same level as the kind of working-class or social demands that come from Marxist laboratories or secular humanism, they can only disenchant those who are fleeing poverty, whereas Christ presents poverty to us as a source of happiness....

It is easy to admit this when you are sheltered from the risk of utter destitution. But when you suffer every day the constraints of insecurity and you are the victim of grave situations of injustice, it may seem strange that anyone should address to us, above all, a call to Transcendence. Among the duties incumbent on Christianity and the Church, the first and the most sacred is not to say pleasant things, but to maintain the purity of the message, which is not about the salvation of man by man, but about the salvation of man by God.[82]

It is time to resort to the means of practicing true priestly poverty. We must not be afraid to look to the experience of religious communities in order to live the virtue of moderation concretely and to share our goods in common. Unless we depend on one another or on the community to live, we cannot embrace fully the mystery of Christ the Priest. Financial autonomy and material security separate us from Him, Who had not even a stone on which to rest His head.

My dear brother priests, let us turn away from the world, from its filth, its luxuries, its proud pretentions, and let us constantly set our sights on Christ. Let us contemplate Him and try to imitate Him. He comes to us without splendor or grandeur or majesty, dressed like the poor man in his humility. May He be our one and only paradigm, our only path to follow.

Benedict XVI recalled this in the book *From the Depths of Our Hearts*, where he laid the foundations for a true reform of the clergy. Very few readers noted the severe demands of his words. Will we dare to listen to him? I know how much Pope Francis appreciated the following words, which he was able to read in the autographed copy that the pope emeritus had sent to him:

[82] "Monde chrétien et monde moderne," in: *Esprit* (1960), quoted in Leon Arthur Elchinger, *Je plaide pour l'homme* (Paris: Fayard, 1976).

Fundamental parts of the priesthood are something like the status of the Levites, exposed, not having land, projected-on-God. The account of vocation in Luke 5:1–11, which we considered first, ends with the words: "They left everything and followed him" (Lk 5:11). Without such a forsaking [of material goods] on our part there is no priesthood. The call to follow is not possible without this sign of freedom and renunciation of any kind of compromise. I think that from this point of view celibacy acquires its great significance as a forgoing of a future earthly home and the leading of one's own life in chosen and familiar surroundings, and that thus it becomes truly indispensable, in order that being given over to God may remain fundamental and become truly realized. This means—it is clear—that celibacy imposes its demands in whatever setting up of one's life. Its full significance cannot be attained if for everything else we follow the rules of property and of life's game as commonly accepted today. It is above all not possible for celibacy to have stability if we do not make remaining close to God the centre of our life.

Psalm 16, like Psalm 119, is a strong pointer to the necessity for continual meditation to make the word of God our own, for only so can we become at home with it and can it become our home. The community aspect of liturgical prayer and worship necessarily connected with this comes out here, where Psalm 16 speaks of the Lord as "my cup" (v. 5). In accordance with the language usual in the Old Testament this reference is to the festive cup which would have been passed round from hand to hand at the sacrificial meal, or to the fatal cup, the cup of wrath or salvation. The New Testament priest who prays the psalm can find indicated here in a special way that chalice by means of which the Lord in the deepest sense has become our land, our inheritance: the Eucharistic Chalice, in which he shares himself with us as our life. The priestly life in the presence of God thus takes on actuality in our life in virtue of the Eucharistic mystery. In the most profound sense, the Eucharist is the land which has become our portion and of which we can say: "The lines have fallen for me in pleasant places; yea, I have a goodly heritage" (v. 6).[83]

---

[83] Benedict XVI and Sarah, *From the Depths of Our Hearts*, 46–47. The passage is taken from a Lenten retreat preached by Cardinal Ratzinger for Pope John Paul II in 1983. The last paragraph is quoted from Joseph Cardinal Ratzinger, *Journey to Easter*, trans. Dame Mary Groves (1987; New York: Crossroad, 2005), 154–155, lightly emended.

IX

Finding One's Place Again

Based on a meditation by Georges Bernanos

Introduction

I wanted to include in this collection of meditations this passage
by a layman, a twentieth-century French novelist, Georges Bernanos. In *Diary of a Country Priest* (*Journal d'un curé de campagne*), the
author states several essential truths about the priesthood. He has
a somewhat bewildered, wavering young priest dialogue with an
old, experienced parish priest, Father de Torcy. The latter pelts his
young confrere with several hard truths: "You do not pray enough.
You suffer too much for the little that you pray.... One must eat
in proportion to one's labors, and our prayer must be on the same
scale as our troubles." This adage reflects years of experience. The
more we suffer, the more vitally necessary prayer is for us. Why?
Because prayer brings us back "to our place in the Gospel." This is
our vocation: we are called to join Jesus somewhere in the gospel.
There is a place where we met Him, where His glance rested on
us. The priest must often return to this place through prayer. He
must often put himself back there, in the sight of Christ. Is this
an image? Maybe. But it is also a spiritual reality. Our personal

vocation opens up for each one of us a place near Jesus. We must rediscover at that place an innocent way of looking, like Mary's. "The Virgin's glance is the only truly childlike glance, the only true glance of a child that has ever been directed toward our shame and our misfortune." Bernanos was able to detect the most intimate feature of the relation between a priest and the Virgin Mary. Why is Mary especially close to priests? Because she is the Mother of the first among them, and more than His Mother: His co-worker in the priestly work of salvation. She sums up in herself alone the whole interior and spiritual aspect of Christ's priestly offering for the world. What is called the baptismal priesthood is, so to speak, summed up and refined in her. The priest participates in this royal priesthood that consists of offering, in prayer, one's love in union with Christ. He, too, needs to feel it. Basically, he is there only to serve this love and to arouse it in the faithful. He does this especially in prayer.

"You do not pray enough!" Father de Torcy scolds his young assistant. Certainly, older and more experienced priests have a sacred duty to initiate young priests into their priestly ministry and to accompany them fraternally by their teaching and counsel and, above all, by their example. However, whether we have a long priestly experience or are young priests, we can never insist enough on the central place of prayer in our lives. Indeed, the prayer of a priest is supposed to continue for the Church the prayer of Jesus in Gethsemane. His whole life, all his activities tend to carry out this essential priestly office of Christ. If only we could understand better each day that the priest's prayer is the first form of the apostolate and the first goal of any priestly vocation!

It is enough for us to observe the life of Jesus, Who, for thirty years in Nazareth, in the silence of His humble, hidden work as a carpenter, listened to God the Father and prayed in the secrecy of

His heart or together with Joseph and the Virgin Mary, His Mother. And before starting His public ministry of evangelization, Jesus withdrew to the solitude and silence of the desert to remain face-to-face with God the Father, to pray and do penance for forty days and forty nights. During His public life, He very often took the time to go, either alone or with His disciples, to a remote place or "to the hills to pray, and all night he continued in prayer to God" (Lk 6:12).

On His last night before His death on the Cross, Jesus went, as usual, to the Garden of Gethsemane. He Who is purity itself, "the Holy One of God," delivered Himself to the torments of sin to carry out the will of His Father, "who desires all men to be saved and to come to the knowledge of the truth" (1 Tim 2:4). On His knees and prostrate on the earth beneath the weight of the sin of the world, He delivered us from it, while praying sorrowfully and more insistently until "his sweat became like great drops of blood falling down upon the ground" (Lk 22:44).

Georges Bernanos, *Diary of a Country Priest*: Old Father de Torcy's advice to his young confrere

"And I fear that the same goes for the interior life, my friend. You do not pray enough. You suffer too much for the little that you pray. That's what I think. One must eat in proportion to one's labors, and our prayer must be on the same scale as our troubles."

"It's just ... I don't ... I can't!" I exclaimed. And immediately I regretted admitting it, because he looked at me sternly.

"If you can't pray, keep trying! Listen, I have gone through my own trials, too. The devil inspired in me such a horror of prayer that I would sweat bullets to say my Rosary. Eh? Try to understand!"

"Oh, I understand," I answered, or rather blurted, so that he examined me for a long time, from feet to head, but without malevolence, on the contrary....

"Listen," he said, "I don't think that I'm mistaken about your case. Try to answer the question that I will ask you. Oh, I'm giving you my little test for what it's worth; this is just my own idea, a way of getting my bearings, and of course it has got me back on track more than once. In short, I have reflected a lot about our vocation. We are all called, true, but not in the same way. And to simplify things, I will start by trying to put each one of us back in his true place, in the Gospel. Oh, of course, that rejuvenates us by two thousand years, and then...! Time is nothing for the good Lord; he sees through it all. I tell myself that, well before our birth (humanly speaking), Our Lord met us somewhere, in Bethlehem, in Nazareth, on the road of Galilee, who knows? On one of those days, his eyes were fixed on us, and depending on the place, the hour, the circumstances, our vocation assumed its particular character. Oh, this is not theology that I am not giving you here! Anyway, I think, I imagine, I dream ... what? That our soul has not forgotten and still remembers, and if she could drag our poor body from one century to another, make it climb that enormous slope of two thousand years, she would lead it right to that same place where ... What? What's the matter? What has come over you?"

I had not noticed that I was weeping, I wasn't thinking about that.

"Why are you crying?"

The truth is that I have always been in the Garden of Olives, and at that moment—yes, it is strange, at the precise moment when he put his hand on Peter's shoulder and asked that question, which was quite useless ultimately, almost naive, but so courteous and tender: "Are you sleeping?" It was a very familiar, very natural movement of my soul; I had not noticed it until then, and suddenly ...

"What has come over you?" Father de Torcy repeated impatiently. "You are not even listening to me, you are dreaming. My friend, someone who wants to pray must not dream. Your prayer trickles away into reverie. There is no symptom more serious for the soul than that hemorrhage!"

I opened my mouth, I was about to reply, but I could not. So much the worse! Was it not enough that Our Lord gave me that grace to reveal to me today, through the mouth of my old master, that nothing would ever remove me from the place chosen for me from all eternity, that I was a prisoner of the Holy Agony? Who would dare to boast about such a grace? I dried my eyes, and I blew my nose so clumsily that Father smiled....

"Work," he said. "Do little things while waiting, day by day. Apply yourself diligently. Remember the pupil bent over the page he is writing, and sticking out his tongue. That is how the good Lord wants to see us when he leaves us to our own devices. The little things seem insignificant, but they give peace. It is like the lilies of the fields, you see. They are thought to have no scent, and yet all together they are fragrant. The prayer of the little things is innocent. In each little thing there is an Angel. Do you pray to the Angels?"

"My God, yes ... of course."

"People do not pray enough to the Angels. They scare theologians somewhat, because of those old heresies in the Eastern Churches, and make them nervous. Well! The world is full of Angels. And the Blessed Virgin: do you pray to the Blessed Virgin?"

"Good heavens!"

"People say that.... But do you pray to her as you should, do you pray to her correctly? She is our mother; everyone understands that. She is the mother of the human race, the New Eve. But she is also its daughter. The ancient world—the sorrowful world, the world as it was before Grace—rocked her for a long time on its desolate heart, for centuries and centuries, in the obscure, incomprehensible expectation of a *virgo genitrix* [virgin-mother]....
For centuries and centuries, with its old hands, its heavy, crime-laden hands, it protected the wonderful little girl, although it did not even know her name. A little girl, this Queen of the Angels. And so she is still, don't forget it! The Middle Ages understood this correctly; the Middle Ages understood everything. But go, then, and prevent the imbeciles from rewriting in their own way the 'drama of the Incarnation,' as they say! Although they think that, for the sake of prestige, they have to dress up unassuming justices of the peace like clowns or sew braids on the sleeves of train conductors, they would be ashamed to admit to unbelievers that the one and only drama, the drama of all dramas—for there is no other—played out without sets and without costumes.

Just think! The Word was made flesh, and the journalists of that time knew nothing about it! Whereas everyday experience teaches them that it is devilishly difficult to recognize the truly great things, even human ones: genius, heroism, love itself—their poor love. So much so that ninety-nine times out of a hundred they will bring their rhetorical flowers to the cemetery; they are bestowed only on the dead. The holiness of God! The simplicity of God, the frightening simplicity of God who damned the pride of the Angels! Yes, the devil must have tried to look it in the face, and the immense, flamboyant torch at the summit of creation was plunged all at once into night. The Jewish people were stiff-necked, otherwise they would have understood that a God who had become man, achieving man's perfection, ran the risk of going unnoticed, that it was necessary to keep their eyes peeled. And just look at the episode of the triumphal entry into Jerusalem; I find it so beautiful! Our Lord deigned to enjoy triumph as he did the rest, as he experienced death; he rejected none of our joys, he only rejected sin. But his death, well, he was meticulous about it, and nothing was missing. Whereas his triumph is a triumph for children, don't you think? A bright-colored Épinal print, with the foal of the donkey, and palm branches, and the people from the countryside clapping their hands. A nice, somewhat ironic parody of imperial pomps. Our Lord looks like he is smiling—Our Lord often smiles. He says to us: 'Don't take these sorts of things too seriously, but still there are legitimate triumphs; it is not forbidden to triumph when Joan of Arc returns to Orléans, under the flowers and the banners, with her beautiful cloak made out of cloth of gold, and I don't want it to be possible for her to think that she is doing wrong. Since you insist on it so much, my poor little children, I sanctified your triumph, I blessed it, as I blessed the wine from your vineyards.' And note well that the same goes for miracles. He works no more of them than necessary. Miracles are the pictures in the book, the beautiful pictures!

But now mark well, lad: the Blessed Virgin had neither a triumph nor miracles. Her Son did not allow human glory to brush against her, not even with the finest tip of its great, wild wing. No one ever lived, or suffered, or died as simply and in such profound ignorance of her own dignity, a dignity that nevertheless sets her above the Angels. After all, she was born without sin: what astonishing uniqueness! Such a pure and limpid spring, so limpid and so pure that she could not even see her own image reflected in it, because it was made to be enjoyed by the Father alone—O sacred solitude! The ancient demons, man's familiar spirits, masters and slaves all together, the terrible patriarchs who guided the first steps of Adam at the threshold of the accursed world—Cunning and Pride—you see them looking from afar at this miraculous creature set beyond their reach, invulnerable and disarmed. Certainly our poor species is worth little, but infancy always stirs its heart, the ignorance of the little one makes it lower its eyes—its eyes which know good and evil, its eyes which have seen so many things! But it is only ignorance after all. The Virgin was Innocence.

Do you realize what we are for her, we others, the human race? Oh, naturally, she detests sin, but she has no experience of it anyway, whereas the greatest saints, even the Saint of Assisi himself, seraphic as he may be, had that experience. The Virgin's glance is the only truly childlike glance, the only true glance of a child that has ever been directed toward our shame and our misfortune. Yes, my lad, in order to pray to her correctly, you have to feel upon you that glance which is not quite a glance of indulgence—because there is no indulgence without some bitter experience—but rather of tender compassion, of sorrowful surprise, of who knows what other inconceivable, inexpressible sentiment that makes her younger than sin, younger than the race from which she stemmed, and although she is our Mother through grace, the Mother of all grace, she is the littlest daughter of the human race."[84]

Meditation

The priesthood is an unprecedented grace that comes to us from God. The priesthood, therefore, is not something that emanates from the community of believers, as many seem to imagine. We are thinking in particular about the crisis in the doctrine on the priesthood that occurred following the Protestant Reformation. Some wanted the priest to be reduced to a mere representative of the community. They wanted to suppress the essential difference between the ordained priesthood and the common priesthood of the faithful. We are thinking also about the spiritual and existential crisis that appeared in the second half of the twentieth century and reached its height chronologically after the Second Vatican Council—but certainly not because of the Council—a crisis from which we still suffer today. In order to be capable of confronting this crisis situation, it is necessary to recall the theological and dogmatic foundations of the Catholic priesthood, from which

[84] Georges Bernanos, *Le Journal d'un curé de campagne* (Paris: Plon, 1936). Translated from French.

several spiritual and pastoral consequences and implications follow immediately. We will not overcome the crisis of the priesthood and, more generally, the crisis of faith that characterizes and swamps our era unless the dogmatic and spiritual foundations and basics of the Catholic Faith and priesthood are recalled and placed at the center of the Church's life and action.

From this perspective, a first fundamental step is the statement that after the Incarnation and the Redemption, the relation between God and mankind is no longer only the one that exists between creatures and the Creator but also the one between adopted children and God the Father, thus passing from the natural order of creation to the supernatural order. A direct consequence of this extraordinary elevation is likewise the elevation of the Catholic priesthood, which can be understood only with a clear reference to the supernatural order of grace. Now it is a participation in the eternal Priesthood of Christ. He, the only true perfect Priest, is the One Who offers perfect worship to the Father through the unique expiatory sacrifice that He offered on the altar of the Cross. Those who receive priestly ordination are priests only through participation in the priesthood of Christ, the Head and Spouse of the Church. They are always envoys to whom Christ Jesus has communicated and entrusted His own mission. Indeed, Jesus established a surprising equality between Him and them. "Truly, truly, I say to you, he who receives any one whom I send receives me; and he who receives me receives him who sent me" (Jn 13:20). This analogy with Christ, however, is by no means the work of the priest himself; it is not due to his own merits. Priests have the sacred power (*sacra potestas*) of communicating the grace of which Jesus alone is the source and which He transmits: the power to forgive the sins that He alone can pardon; to offer to God the worship that He alone can offer. Although it is true that every

Christian accomplishes, with the help of grace, everything that is possible for him to do and for which he is competent by virtue of his Baptism and Confirmation, the priest and only the priest, through priestly ordination, is made capable of doing what he is radically incapable of doing by himself.

Thus, the priesthood is a grace and a sacred power received from Christ. Only Jesus Christ can do in the priest what the priest does every day in the Church. The priest who consecrates and offers the sacrifice is therefore not the mere representative or the mere spokesman of those who attend and participate to a certain extent in the celebration of the Mystery. He is indeed that, too, in certain actions,

> even in liturgical actions, for the liturgy includes a whole section of worship ascending from men to God; but in the strictly sacramental actions of the liturgy, and especially in the consecration of the eucharistic offerings, the priest celebrates primarily the cultus of the Lord and is primarily the minister and sacramental representative of Christ; he celebrates, says theology, *in persona Christi*.[85]

Thus, when we celebrate the Holy Sacrifice of the Mass, the great Christian prayer, we consecrate the bread and the wine "*in persona Christi*," after handing over to Him our bodies, our voices, and our hearts, which have been sullied so many times by numerous sins, and which we ask Him to purify. Already on the day before each of our Eucharistic celebrations, we are snuggled like children in the arms of the Virgin Mary, and she herself prepares and leads us to commend ourselves, body and soul, to Jesus Christ,

---

[85] Yves Congar, "Structure du sacerdoce chrétien," cited in de Lubac, *The Splendor of the Church*, 141.

so that the miracle of the Eucharist may be accomplished. The Cross, the Host, and the Virgin Mary fashion, structure, feed, and strengthen our Christian and priestly life. You understand why every Christian, and more particularly the priest, must build his interior life on these three pillars: *Crux, Hostia, et Virgo.* The Cross, the Eucharist, and the Virgin.

The Cross has truly become a source of infinite benefits: it has freed us from error, dispelled our darkness, and reconciled us with God. This Cross is the destruction of enmity, the source of peace, our treasure chest, Saint John Chrysostom writes. And Benedict XVI echoes him when he says that

> the Cross is not the banner of the victory of death, sin, and evil, but rather the luminous sign of Love, of God's immense Love, of something that we could never have asked, imagined, or expected: God bent down over us, he lowered himself, even to the darkest corner of our lives, in order to stretch out his hand and draw us to Himself, to bring us all the way to Himself. The Cross speaks to us of the supreme Love of God and invites [us], today, to renew our faith in the power of that love, and to believe that in every situation of our lives, our history and our world, God is able to vanquish death, sin, and evil, and to give us new, risen life. In the Son of God's death on the cross, we find the seed of new hope for life, like the seed which dies within the earth.[86]

The Cross causes us to be born to divine life. In contemplating it, we learn to pray and to forgive. For from the height of the

[86] Address of His Holiness Pope Benedict XVI after the Stations of the Cross at the Colosseum, April 22, 2011.

Cross we hear Jesus praying and offering Himself totally to God the Father: "'Father, forgive them; for they know not what they do.' ... 'Father, into your hands I commit my spirit!' And having said this he breathed his last" (Lk 23:34, 46).

The Eucharist is the life of our lives. "Without the Eucharist we cannot live." The center of the Church and the center of the life of every Christian is the Eucharist. In order to celebrate the Eucharist worthily, we must fall on our knees, prostrate ourselves, adore, and allow ourselves to be purified, transformed, transfigured by the mystery of the condescension of God, Who comes to us by humbling Himself to our level so as to raise us to His height and to His holiness. When we eat His Body and drink His Blood, Jesus makes us become Himself. He abides in us and we in Him. He divinizes us and makes us live with His life.

As for the Virgin Mary, she attentively watches over our spiritual development, educates us to grow in faith and love, and facilitates our union with God. Mary leads us more easily to Jesus and teaches us to love and serve Him humbly with our whole heart. Mary is our sure refuge. She intervenes more swiftly and more tenderly than any other earthly mother to help us in our trials and to give us the appropriate assistance.

And so Saint Louis-Marie de Montfort can declare in his *Treatise on True Devotion*:

> It is quite true that we can attain to divine union by other roads, but these involve many more crosses and exceptional setbacks and many difficulties that we cannot easily overcome. We would have to pass through spiritual darkness, engage in struggle for which we are not prepared, endure bitter agonies, scale precipitous mountains, tread upon painful thorns, and cross frightful deserts. But when we

take the path of Mary, we walk smoothly and calmly. It is true that on our way we have hard battles to fight and serious obstacles to overcome, but Mary, our Mother and Queen, stays close to her faithful servants. She is always at hand to brighten their darkness, clear away their doubts, strengthen them in their fears, sustain them in their combats and trials. Truly, in comparison with other ways, this virgin road to Jesus is a path of roses and sweet delights.[87]

Georges Bernanos has good reason to write that

The Virgin's glance is the only truly childlike glance, the only true glance of a child that has ever been directed toward our shame and our misfortune. Yes, my lad, in order to pray to her correctly, you have to feel upon you that glance which is not quite a glance of indulgence—because there is no indulgence without some bitter experience—but rather of tender compassion, of sorrowful surprise, of who knows what other inconceivable, inexpressible sentiment that makes her younger than sin, younger than the race from which she stemmed, and although she is our Mother through grace, the Mother of all grace, she is the littlest daughter of the human race.

These passages by Georges Bernanos and Saint Louis-Marie de Montfort state magnificently and confidently the great importance of recourse to the Blessed Virgin Mary, our good Mother in our anxieties and difficulties, and the maternal, luminous mission that is hers in the Church. Like the Apostles in the Cenacle, let us

---

[87] St. Louis de Montfort, *True Devotion to the Blessed Virgin*, chap. IV, art. 5, §1 = par. 152 (Bay Shore, New York: Montfort Publications, 1987), 74.

place ourselves under her virginal mantle and under the lightning rod of her daily intercession. May Mary obtain for us the graces that we need most for our sanctification and for the spread of the Church's work. May she obtain for us above all love, her immense love, which gave her the grace to bear in her womb the Son of God, so that we might be capable of carrying out the mission of bringing Jesus Christ to souls. May she teach us to be pure and chaste, as she was. May she make us faithful to our priestly vocation, make us savor all the beauty, the joy, and the strength of a ministry and a mission that are lived out unreservedly and with devotion in our daily self-sacrifice in the service of God and of souls. May Mary help us to say at every moment and after her example the great word *Fiat*, "yes," to God's will, even when it is demanding and uncompromising. We know that she stands at the foot of our cross and supports us tenderly by her prayer.

In mentioning Mary's glance at the priest, Bernanos uses the word "compassion." I think that we must understand it in a strong sense. Not only is Mary not indifferent to the joys and sorrows of a man who has become a priest, but, more profoundly, she suffers with him; she enters with him into that passion, just as she accompanied Christ on Calvary. Her motherhood is revealed there in its fullness. At the Cross, Saint John, the apostle and priest, receives Mary as his mother. She encourages us at every moment to live out our priesthood in its fullness. She lifts us up when we fall and tells us continually: "Go up higher; dare to go even to Golgotha. That is where souls are saved. That is where Jesus, my Son, the eternal priest ransoms the world."

In a married couple, the wife is often the one who pays attention to the details, to the humblest and hidden aspects. Women have the genius of simplicity. They see precisely the discreet, hidden, and secret things. Men tend to think that the only important thing is what is noticed at first. The Virgin Mary gives to the priest the ability not to neglect any detail of his life. She teaches him that nothing should escape his priestly tact. It seems to me that prayer to Mary, prayer with Mary, through the daily recitation of the Rosary, introduces into the life of a celibate priest a necessary motherly presence. This is not a matter of emotional or psychological compensation. But we know that manliness needs to be refined through contact with the feminine sensibility. This spiritual contact with Mary balances the soul of a priest and makes it deeper and more refined. Mary is the mother and the instructress of priestly souls. She watches daily over the interior joy of her priests.

X

Priest and Victim

Based on a meditation by Saint John Henry Newman

Introduction

"My wish is to be separated from everything of this world; to cleanse myself simply from sin; to put away from me even what is innocent, if used for its own sake, and not for Thine. I put away reputation and honour, and influence, and power, for my praise and strength shall be in Thee."[88]

This prayer of Saint John Henry Newman reveals his priestly heart. Reputation, honor, influence, and power are so many snares for the priestly soul. They are like will-o'-the-wisps, the illusory lights in antiquity that misled mariners toward reefs and caused shipwrecks. How can a priest detach himself definitively from these temptations? His vocation sets him in front of the people of God. He must often speak. Sometimes it is his responsibility to unravel tangled situations. How could reputation and influence not be attractive? How can he avoid attributing some power to himself under

---

[88] John Henry Cardinal Newman, *Meditations on Christian Doctrine* (London: Longmans, Green, 1908), 108.

the guise of good intentions? Newman answers us very clearly: it is enough to put into practice what we profess. Now, what we profess is first and foremost the Mass. At the altar, Christ makes use of our words to make present and to actualize His unique sacrifice. The Cross is the sacrifice that reconciles us with God because, in it, the Victim and the Priest are one body. The One Who offers is the One Who is offered. When a priest offers the Sacrifice of the Mass, he does so in the first person: "This is my body." He is sacramentally identified with Christ, Who offers. The priest at the altar, therefore, must offer himself, too, as a victim on the Cross.

There, on the Cross, at the altar, the priest is truly himself. That is where he extends his arms to let himself, too, be nailed to the wood. In short, that is where his hands will be pierced so as to retain nothing, so as to be delivered from the temptation to be grasping. Our priestly hands must not take but, rather, must offer. The good that we do is not our property. The souls we help are not ours. They pass through us to go to God, as God passes through us to go to souls. We are only instruments. During Mass, at the altar, we become aware of this again. We experience our nothingness before the greatness of God. We become lost in Him, in His sacrifice, like the drop of water in the Precious Blood in the chalice.

If we do not mount the Cross each day, we run the risk of making the altar the vain, illusory throne of our ego, of our glory. In the liturgy, when a priest chatters, comments, and incessantly adds human words to those of the Church, he demonstrates his unwillingness to be self-effacing in the presence of the Word. He wants people to look at him, a petty human person, to listen to him, to be interested in him. At the altar, the priest must wish to disappear, to be forgotten, to hide in the Church's words and in Christ's. He ought to tremble with fear and astonishment at the divine majesty and hide under the mantle of the Church.

There, forgotten by everyone, he will let Christ appear through him. Then he will be at his place. O priest, remember that you will be yourself only when you are truly a victim.

Dear confreres in the priesthood, we disappear from the world's sight if Jesus Christ wholly takes first place during our celebration of the Eucharist, if we immerse ourselves in prayer and if our life is "hidden with Christ in God" (Col 3:3). Mass is the prayer par excellence, the high point of our encounter with Our Lord. However, we run the risk of its becoming for us merely a cold ritual, repeated thousands of times. No! Dear priest friends! We must pray during Mass; in other words, we must communicate with God, converse intimately with Him and not only with the people who are in front of us. We must be able to see Him with our own eyes, touch Him, contemplate His presence. Let us ask ourselves, let each one of us pose the question: When I celebrate Mass, do I pray? Do I address God? Do I really speak with God? Do I look at Him face-to-face? Do I let Him look at me?

Saint John Henry Newman,
Meditations on Christian Doctrine

The Holy Sacrifice of the Mass

I adore Thee, O my Lord God, with the most profound awe for Thy passion and crucifixion, in sacrifice for our sins. Thou didst suffer incommunicable sufferings in Thy sinless soul. Thou wast exposed in Thy innocent body to ignominious torments, to mingled pain and shame. Thou wast stripped and fiercely scourged, Thy sacred body vibrating under the heavy flail as trees under the blast. Thou wast, when thus mangled, hung up upon the Cross, naked, a spectacle for all to see Thee quivering and dying. What does all this imply, O Mighty God! What a depth is here which we cannot fathom! My God, I know well, Thou couldst have saved us at Thy word, without Thyself suffering; but Thou didst choose to purchase us at the price of Thy Blood. I look on Thee, the Victim lifted up on Calvary, and I know and protest that that death of Thine was an expiation for the sins of the whole world. I believe and know, that Thou alone couldst have offered a meritorious atonement; for it was Thy Divine Nature which gave Thy sufferings worth. Rather then than I should perish according to my deserts, Thou wast nailed to the Tree and didst die.

Such a sacrifice was not to be forgotten. It was not to be — it could not be — a mere event in the world's history, which was to be done and over, and was to pass away except in its obscure, unrecognised effects. If that great deed was what we believe it to be, what we know it is, it must remain present, though past; it must be a standing fact for all times. Our own careful reflection upon it tells us this; and there-fore, when we are told that Thou, O Lord, though Thou hast ascended to glory, hast renewed and perpetuated Thy sacrifice to the end of all things, not only is the news most touching and joyful, as testifying to so tender a Lord and Saviour, but it carries with it the full assent and sympathy of our reason. Though we neither could, nor would have dared, anticipate so wonderful a doctrine, yet we adore its very suitableness to Thy perfections, as well as its infinite compassionateness for us, now that we are told of it. Yes, my Lord, though Thou hast left the world, Thou art daily offered up in the Mass; and, though Thou canst not suffer

pain and death, Thou dost still subject Thyself to indignity
and restraint to carry out to the full Thy mercies towards
us. Thou dost humble Thyself daily; for, being infinite,
Thou couldst not end Thy humiliation while they existed
for whom Thou didst submit to it. So Thou remainest a
Priest for ever.

My Lord, I offer Thee myself in turn as a sacrifice of
thanksgiving. Thou hast died for me, and I in turn make
myself over to Thee. I am not my own. Thou hast bought
me; I will by my own act and deed complete the purchase.
My wish is to be separated from everything of this world;
to cleanse myself simply from sin; to put away from me
even what is innocent, if used for its own sake, and not for
Thine. I put away reputation and honour, and influence,
and power, for my praise and strength shall be in Thee.
Enable me to carry out what I profess.[89]

Book of Prayers: Prayer of Trust in God

God created me to do Him some definite service; He has
committed some work to me which He has not committed
to another. I have my mission — I never may know it in this
life, but I shall be told it in the next. . . . I am a link in a
chain, a bond of connexion between persons. He has not
created me for naught. I shall do good, I shall do His work;
I shall be . . . a preacher of the truth in my own place, while
not intending it, if I do but keep His commandments and
serve Him in my calling. . . .

O my God, I will put myself without reserve into Thy
hands. . . . What have I in heaven, and apart from Thee what

---

[89] *Meditations on Christian Doctrine*, 106–108.

want I upon earth? My flesh and my heart faileth: but God
is the God of my heart, and my portion for ever.[90]

Meditation

Before any activity, in the early morning, we must turn to the Lord,
our Creator, and plead in the presence of the Most High. Before
any apostolic commitment, every morning and in the course of
the day, this poor priest that I am must enter and disappear into
the mystery of the Holy Eucharist, celebrated fervently and contemplated and adored at length. This little Host, which bears the
whole world, the entire universe, and all of human history, must
become the center of our existence, the life of our lives. We must
offer ourselves to God as a sacrifice and be transformed into this
Host, allow ourselves to be transubstantiated, so to speak, and to
become Christ Himself. Saint Peter Chrysologus confirms this in
his homily on spiritual sacrifice:

> Listen now to what the Apostle urges us to do. "I appeal to
> you," he says, "to present your bodies as a living sacrifice."
> By this exhortation of his, Paul has raised all men to priestly
> status. How marvelous is the priesthood of the Christian,
> for he is both the victim that is offered on his own behalf,
> and the priest who makes the offering. He does not need to
> go beyond himself to seek what he is to immolate to God:
> with himself and in himself he brings the sacrifice he is to
> offer God for himself. The victim remains and the priest
> remains, always one and the same. Immolated, the victim

[90] *Meditations on Christian Doctrine*, 5, 4.

still lives: the priest who immolates cannot kill. Truly it is an amazing sacrifice in which a body is offered without being slain and blood is offered without being shed.

The Apostle says: "I appeal to you by the mercy of God to present your bodies as a living sacrifice" (Rom 12:1). Brethren, this sacrifice follows the pattern of Christ's sacrifice by which he gave his body as a living immolation for the life of the world. He really made his body a living sacrifice, because, though slain, he continues to live....

The prophet said the same thing: "Sacrifice and offering you did not desire, but you have prepared a body for me" [Heb 10:5, citing Ps 40:6]. Each of us is called to be both a sacrifice to God and his priest. Do not forfeit what divine authority confers on you. Put on the garment of holiness, gird yourself with the belt of chastity. Let Christ be your helmet, let the cross on your forehead be your unfailing protection. Your breastplate should be the knowledge of God that he himself has given you. Keep burning continually the sweet-smelling incense of prayer. Take up the sword of the Spirit. Let your heart be an altar. Then, with full confidence in God, present your body for sacrifice. God desires not death, but faith; God thirsts not for blood, but for self-surrender; God is appeased not by slaughter, but by the offering of your free will.[91]

We must spend our whole lives as priests discovering this immense treasure of the Eucharistic Sacrifice that Jesus gave us so that we ourselves might become Eucharist and thus hide ourselves

[91] Saint Peter Chrysologus, "Homily on Spiritual Sacrifice," in *The Liturgy of the Hours*, vol. 2 (New York: Catholic Book Publishing, 1976), 771–772.

in Jesus. Only then will we be able to give ourselves, too, as Christ did, by accomplishing the Father's will in its entirety. Let us try to imitate Saint Thomas Aquinas: as a man of prayer and contemplation, he always maintained a very lively sense of the absolute primacy of God in all things. Yet this did not cause him to lose the immense intellectual and pedagogical investment in the divine mysteries: "Every time he decided to undertake a debate, to teach, write, or dictate," one of his biographers relates, "he withdrew in the silence and secrecy of prayer and shed tears while praying, so as to obtain an understanding of the divine mysteries."[92] Saint John the Evangelist, that great contemplative and mystic, rested his head on the heart of Jesus during the Last Supper at the moment of the institution of the priesthood and of the Eucharist (Jn 13:23-25). He, too, handed on to others only what he had heard and seen with his own eyes, what he had contemplated and touched in the Word of Life (1 Jn 1:1-4).

Indeed, with the Holy Eucharist, the sacrament that we could call the sacrament of divine generosity, God grants us His grace. God gives Himself to us in Jesus Christ, Who is really and always present in it—not only during Holy Mass, but also in the tabernacle—in His Body and Blood, Soul, and Divinity. Now, thanks to our priestly ordination, we have the vocation and the duty to perpetuate every day, alone or in the presence of the People of God, the Eucharistic Sacrifice, the sacrifice of the gift that Jesus makes of Himself to the Father. And after adoring and contemplating Him, we must give this presence of love to the faithful so that they may feed on it. Through the imposition of hands, we

[92] Guglielmo da Tocco, *Histoire de Saint Thomas d'Aquin*, translated into French and edited by Claire Le Brun-Gouanvic, "Sagesse chrétienne" (Paris: Éditions du Cerf, 2005).

have received on our souls an indelible character that configures us to Christ the Priest, Head of the Mystical Body. Therefore, we have to work or, rather, allow ourselves to be shaped each day, so that, thanks to the Holy Spirit, we might perfectly resemble Christ. The resemblance is like the one that exists between the water that springs from the source and the water that has come from it in a jug. Indeed, by nature, it is the same purity that we see in Christ and in the one who participates in Christ. But in Christ, it springs from the source, and the one who participates in Christ draws from that source the purity and beauty of Christ and brings it into his life.[93] A wondrous mystery, but how formidable and terrifying at the same time. The mystery of our priesthood should fill us with astonishment and trembling, but at the same time with a great joy.

By the Sacrament of Holy Orders, in pronouncing the words of the Consecration, which are the very words of Christ, we consecrate the bread and the wine so that they become the Body and Blood of Christ. In this way, we offer to God the Holy Sacrifice. We can forgive sins in sacramental Confession and perform the noble ministry of teaching doctrine to the people. You see, dear brothers, that in the priesthood all that we are, all that we do, all that we say or teach does not belong to us. Everything, absolutely everything, is a gift and manifestation of the Love of God for the benefit of human beings through our poor and humble persons and without any merit on our part. We are priests in order to reveal the God of Love, who manifested Himself on the Cross, and to arouse, by means of prayer: faith, the conversion of hearts, true love, and the return of sinful man to God.

---

[93] See Cyril of Jerusalem, *Catechetical Lectures*, 22, 3 [NPNF 2, 7:151b]. [The author paraphrases.]

For us as priests, pastors, and guides of the People of God, our constant preoccupation must be unfailing loyalty to Christ's teaching. As Tertullian testifies, we must teach nothing other than what Christ's Apostles taught. They

> went out into the whole world and proclaimed to the nations the same doctrinal faith. They set up churches in every city. Other churches received from them a living transplant of faith and the seed of doctrine, and through this daily process of transplanting they became churches. They therefore qualify as apostolic churches by being the offspring of the churches that are apostolic.[94]

Let us then fight constantly to acquire a delicate conscience, fidelity, and a religious respect for the dogma and the morality that make up the deposit of faith and the common patrimony of Christ's Church. This is precisely the advice and the exhortation that Saint Paul addresses to each of us when he writes to Timothy:

> Till I come, attend to the public reading of Scripture, to preaching, to teaching. Do not neglect the gift you have, which was given you by prophetic utterance when the elders laid their hands upon you. Practice these duties, devote yourself to them.... Take heed to yourself and to your teaching; hold to that, for by so doing you will save both yourself and your hearers. (1 Tim 4:13-16)

If we are afraid to proclaim the truth of the Gospel, if we are intimidated and fear the criticism and the attacks of the secularist world, if we are ashamed of denouncing serious deviations in the

---

[94] Tertullian, *On the Prescription of Heretics*, in *The Liturgy of the Hours*, 2:1811.

domain of doctrine and morality, and if we adapt to this world, then the prophetic words of Ezekiel will fall on us like a severe divine rebuke:

> Ho, shepherds of Israel who have been feeding yourselves! Should not shepherds feed the sheep? You eat the fat, you clothe yourselves with the wool, you slaughter the fatlings, but you do not feed the sheep. The weak you have not strengthened, the sick you have not healed, the crippled you have not bound up, the strayed you have not brought back, the lost you have not sought, and with force and harshness you have ruled them. (Ezek 34:2–4)

These are serious rebukes, but even more serious is the offense that one would commit against God if, having freely received the responsibility to watch over the spiritual good of all, we mistreated souls by giving them confused, ambiguous, and relativistic personal opinions and deprived them of the doctrine revealed by God and transmitted by the Church.

He who does not fight to preach the gospel, to convert, feed, and lead the people of God on the path of truth and life that is Jesus Himself, he who remains silent out of fear, out of shame or human respect in view of the lethal deviations of this world, exposes himself to one or another of these slaveries that can fetter our poor hearts: the slavery of an exclusively human and horizontal view of things, the slavery of an ardent desire for power, reputation, or temporal prestige, the slavery of vanity, the slavery of money, and the servitude of sensuality and sexuality gone astray [*dévoyée*]. As John Henry Newman reminds us, we must "put away [= renounce] reputation and honour, and influence, and power." But there is only one way that can free us from these forms of slavery and lead us to carry out fully our ministry as pastors and shepherds: it is the way of love. Love is the key to understanding Christ, resembling Him, and living in communion with His suffering and becoming conformed to Him in His death. He who performs pastoral ministry in the Church can draw his energies only from a supreme love for Christ. To feed the flock is an act of love, and the Mass is its highest expression.

XI

The Priest: A Consecrated Man, a Man of the Sacred

Based on a meditation by Benedict XVI

Introduction

"Our being priests is simply a new and radical way of being united to Christ. In its substance, it has been bestowed on us for ever in the sacrament. But this new seal imprinted upon our being can become for us a condemnation, if our lives do not develop by entering into the truth of the Sacrament." On Holy Thursday morning in 2009, during the Chrism Mass, the frail, slightly trembling voice of Benedict XVI resounded nevertheless with unequaled strength in Saint Peter's Basilica. In a few words, the pope had just summarized the heart of the mystery being lived out by all the men who were gathered around the altar of the Eucharistic Sacrifice, some of whom were not yet thirty years old, while others were approaching death. It was a moment of grace. Benedict XVI opened his heart. Behind the great modesty of the delicate man, one could see the mystery of his soul.

What was he telling us? The priest is radically consecrated, entirely immersed in God's intimacy. Are we really consecrated to

God? Generally, we reserve this term for men and women religious. And yet Benedict XVI explained very clearly: the priest is removed from the profane sphere, from the common sphere, so as to be given to God, so as to be offered as a sacrifice to God. To be consecrated means, therefore, to be taken away from the world; it means to leave the context of worldly life so as to be given absolutely to God. It is to be set apart so as to represent the others in His presence—not because of his merits or his exceptional qualifications but by vocation, by a personal call from God. Every priest heard this call one day resonate in the innermost depths of his soul. And God's voice invited us to leave the world and to leave ourselves so as to cease belonging to ourselves and to be totally His. God clearly addressed these questions to us: Do you want to belong wholly to me? Do you want to be my priest? Do you want to be offered as I am offered? It is good for each of us priests to recall those moments when we met Christ's gaze at us. "And you? Do you also want to belong to me alone?" We answered yes, and our response was like an echo of Jesus' yes to the Father. "Consecrate them in the truth," Jesus said. For His disciples and for each of us, Christ asks for the true sanctification that transforms our being and transforms us in our innermost depths; He asks that this may not remain merely ritual but may be a genuine appropriation of our whole person by God Himself. Above all, He wants this transformation to be achieved day after day in us, to be expressed concretely in our lives, and to make His presence visible and influential in us. So that in seeing us, people will see Christ; so that in hearing us, they will hear Christ; and so that in touching us, they will feel this sacred strength, this physical emanation that went out from Jesus and worked cures (see Mk 5:30).

What is sacred in us is not our poor human person but, rather, our identification with Christ, this yes that we pronounced in Him.

We are consecrated—that is, offered to God. I like to meditate on the letters of John Paul II to priests and especially on the letter *Dominicae Cenae* from Holy Thursday in 1980:

> The sacredness [*Sacrum*] of the Mass, therefore, is not a "sacralization," that is to say, something that man adds to Christ's action in the Upper Room, for the Holy Thursday supper was a sacred rite, a primary and constitutive liturgy, through which Christ, by pledging to give His life for us, Himself celebrated sacramentally the mystery of His passion and resurrection, the heart of every Mass. Our Masses, being derived from this liturgy, possess of themselves a complete liturgical form, which, in spite of its variations in line with the families of rites, remains substantially the same. The sacred character [*Sacrum*] of the Mass is a sacredness instituted by Christ. The words and actions of every priest, answered by the conscious active participation of the whole eucharistic assembly, echo the words and actions of Holy Thursday.
>
> The priest offers the holy Sacrifice *in persona Christi*; this means more than offering "in the name of" or "in place of" Christ. *In persona* means in specific sacramental identification with "the eternal High Priest"[95] who is the author and principal subject of this sacrifice of His, a sacrifice in which, in truth, nobody can take His place. Only He—only Christ—was able and is always able to be the true and effective "expiation for our sins and ... for the sins of the whole world." Only His sacrifice—and no one else's—was

---

[95] Collect from the Votive Mass of the Blessed Sacrament., B. *Missale Romanum.*

able and is able to have a "propitiatory power" before God, the Trinity, and the transcendent holiness. Awareness of this reality throws a certain light on the character and significance of the priest celebrant who, by confecting the holy Sacrifice and acting "*in persona Christi*," is sacramentally (and ineffably) brought into that most profound sacredness, and made part of it, spiritually linking with it in turn all those participating in the eucharistic assembly.

This sacred rite [*Sacrum*], which is actuated in different liturgical forms, may lack some secondary elements, but it can in no way lack its essential sacred character and sacramentality, since these are willed by Christ and transmitted and regulated by the Church. Neither can this sacred rite be utilized for other ends. If separated from its distinctive sacrificial and sacramental nature, the Eucharistic Mystery simply ceases to be. It admits of no "profane" imitation, an imitation that would very easily (indeed regularly) become a profanation. This must always be remembered, perhaps above all in our time, when we see a tendency to do away with the distinction between the "sacred" and "profane," given the widespread tendency, at least in some places, to desacralize everything....

The sacred character of the Eucharist has found and continues to find expression in the terminology of theology and the liturgy.[96] This sense of the objective sacred

[96] We speak about the "*divinum mysterium*," the "*sanctissimum*," or the "*sacrosanctum*"—in other words, about what is "sacred" or "holy" par excellence. For their part, the Eastern Churches call the Mass "*raza*," that is, "*mystérion*," "*hagiasmos*," "*quddasha*," "*qedassé*," that is, "consecration" par excellence. Then there are the liturgical rites that, in order to inspire the sense of the sacred, sometimes

character of the Eucharistic Mystery is so much part of the faith of the People of God that their faith is enriched and strengthened by it. Therefore the ministers of the Eucharist must, especially today, be illumined by the fullness of this living faith, and in its light they must understand and perform all that is part, by Christ's will and the will of His Church, of their priestly ministry.[97]

The priest is consecrated; he is a man of the sacred, because he belongs to God. Some have misinterpreted this reality. They have concluded from it that every act performed by a priest would automatically be good, too. However, as we know, we are capable of sinning. The sacred character of the priest does not make him immune to temptation and evil. He is not preserved from them. On the contrary, every time he falls into sin, his offense is, so to speak, a "sacrilege," and he profanes the fact that he belongs to Christ. His sin has a more serious, more scandalous, more incomprehensible character.

We know that through the sacrament [of Holy Orders] we belong substantially to Christ, but it is up to us every day of our lives to implement this belonging through the spiritual combat.

For good reasons, Christians expect the life of priests to be consistent with the sacred character of their profound identity.

---

demand silence, a standing or kneeling position, or the profession of faith, the incensing of the Gospel, the altar, and the sacred species. Moreover, these rites call for the help of the angelic beings, who were created for the service of the Holy God: through the "*Sanctus*" in our Latin Churches, or through the *Trisagion* and the "*sancta sanctis*" [the acclamation "holy things for the holy"] in the Eastern liturgies.

[97] John Paul II, Letter *Dominicae Cenae* on the Mystery and Worship of the Eucharist (February 24, 1980), no. 8.

They know intuitively that a priest who is not a saint is a sort of anomaly, for the sacred without holiness has no meaning.

———⟨∞⟩———

Pope Benedict XVI, Homily at the Chrism Mass, Holy Thursday, April 9, 2009

Dear Brothers and Sisters,

In the Upper Room, on the eve of his Passion, the Lord prayed for his disciples gathered about him. At the same time, he looked ahead to the community of disciples of all centuries, "those who believe in me through their word" (Jn 17:20). In his prayer for the disciples of all time, he saw us too, and he prayed for us. Let us listen to what he asks for the Twelve and for us gathered here: "Sanctify them in the truth; your word is truth. As you sent me into the world, so I have sent them into the world. And for their sake I consecrate myself, so that they also may be consecrated in truth" (Jn 17:17–19). The Lord asks for our sanctification, our consecration in truth. And he sends us forth to carry on his own mission. But in this prayer there is one word which draws our attention, and appears difficult to understand. Jesus says: "For their sake I consecrate myself." What does this mean? Is Jesus not himself "the Holy One of God," as Peter acknowledged at that decisive moment in Capharnaum (cf. Jn 6:69)? How can he now consecrate—sanctify—himself?

To understand this, we need first to clarify what the Bible means by the words "holy" and "sanctify-consecrate." "Holy"—this word describes above all God's own nature, his completely unique, divine way of being, one which is his alone. He alone is the true and authentic Holy One, in the original sense of the word. All other holiness derives from him, is a participation in his way of being. He is purest Light, Truth, and untainted Good. To consecrate something or someone means, therefore, to give that thing or person to God as his property, to take it out of the context of what is ours and to insert it in his milieu, so that it no longer belongs to our affairs, but is totally of God. Consecration is thus a taking away from the world and a giving over to the living God. The thing or person no longer belongs to us, or even to itself, but is immersed in God. Such a giving up of something in order to give it over to God, we also call a sacrifice: this thing will no longer be my property, but his property. In the Old Testament, the giving over of a person to God, his "sanctification," is identified with priestly ordination, and this also defines the essence of the priesthood: it is a transfer of ownership, a being taken out of the world and given to God. We can now see the two directions which belong to the process of sanctification-consecration. It is a departure from the milieux of worldly life—a "being set apart" for God. But for this very reason it is not a segregation. Rather, being given over to God means being charged to represent others. The priest is removed from worldly bonds and given over to God, and precisely in this way, starting with God, he must be available for others, for everyone. When Jesus says: "I consecrate myself," he makes himself both priest and victim. Bultmann was right to translate the phrase: "I consecrate myself" by "I sacrifice myself." Do we now see what happens when Jesus says: "I consecrate myself for them"? This is the priestly act by which Jesus—the Man Jesus, who is one with the Son of God—gives himself over to the Father for us. It is the expression of the fact that he is both priest and victim. I consecrate myself—I sacrifice myself: this unfathomable word, which gives us a glimpse deep into the heart of Jesus Christ, should be the object of constantly renewed reflection. It contains the whole mystery of our redemption. It also contains the origins of the priesthood in the Church, of our priesthood.

Only now can we fully understand the prayer which the Lord offered the Father for his disciples—for us. "Sanctify them in the truth": this is the inclusion of the Apostles in the priesthood of Jesus Christ, the institution of his new priesthood for the community of the faithful of all times. "Sanctify them in truth": this is the true prayer of consecration for the Apostles. The Lord prays that God himself draw them towards him, into his holiness. He prays that God take them away from themselves to make them his own property, so that, starting from him, they can carry out the priestly ministry for the world. This prayer of Jesus appears twice in slightly different forms. Both times we need to listen very carefully, in order to understand, even dimly, the sublime reality that is about to be accomplished. "Sanctify them in the truth." Jesus adds: "Your word is truth." The disciples are thus drawn deep within God by being immersed in the word of God. The word of God is, so to speak, the bath which purifies them, the creative power which transforms them into God's own being. So then, how do things stand in our own lives? Are we truly pervaded by the word of God? Is that word truly the nourishment we live by, even more than bread and the things of this world? Do we really know that word? Do we love it?

Are we deeply engaged with this word to the point that it really leaves a mark on our lives and shapes our thinking? Or is it rather the case that our thinking is constantly being shaped by all the things that others say and do? Aren't prevailing opinions the criterion by which we all too often measure ourselves? Do we not perhaps remain, when all is said and done, mired in the superficiality in which people today are generally caught up? Do we allow ourselves truly to be deeply purified by the word of God? Nietzsche scoffed at humility and obedience as the virtues of slaves, a source of repression. He replaced them with pride and man's absolute freedom. Of course there exist caricatures of a misguided humility and a mistaken submissiveness, which we do not want to imitate. But there also exists a destructive pride and a presumption which tear every community apart and result in violence. Can we learn from Christ the correct humility which corresponds to the truth of our being, and the obedience which submits to truth, to the will of God? "Sanctify them in the truth; your word is truth": this word of inclusion in the priesthood lights up our lives and calls us to become ever anew disciples of that truth which is revealed in the word of God.

We can advance another step in the interpretation of these words. Did not Christ say of himself: "I am the truth" (cf. Jn 14:6)? Is he not himself the living Word of God, to which every other word refers? Sanctify them in the truth—this means, then, in the deepest sense: make them one with me, Christ. Bind them to me. Draw them into me. Indeed, when all is said and done, there is *only one* priest of the New Covenant, Jesus Christ himself. Consequently, the priesthood of the disciples can only be a participation in the priesthood of Jesus. Our being priests is simply a new and radical way of being united to Christ. In its substance, it has been bestowed on us for ever in the sacrament. But this new seal imprinted upon our being can become for us a condemnation, if our lives do not develop by entering into the truth of the Sacrament. The promises we renew today state in this regard that our will must be directed along this path: "*Domino Iesu arctius coniungi et conformari, vobismetipsis abrenuntiantes.*" [To be more closely joined and conformed to the Lord Jesus, while renouncing yourselves.] Being united to Christ calls for renunciation. It means not wanting to impose our own way and our own will, not desiring to become someone else, but abandoning ourselves to him, however and wherever he wants to use us. As Saint Paul said: "It is no longer I who live, but Christ who lives in me" (Gal 2:20). In the words "I do," spoken at our priestly ordination, we made this fundamental renunciation of our desire to be independent, "self-made." But day by day this great "yes" has to be lived out in the many little "yeses" and small sacrifices. This "yes" made up of tiny steps, which together make up the great "yes," can be lived out without bitterness and self-pity only if Christ is truly the center of our lives. If we enter into true closeness to him. Then indeed we experience, amid sacrifices which can at first be painful, the growing joy of friendship with him, and all the small and sometimes great signs of his love, which he is constantly showing us. "The one who loses himself, finds himself." When we dare to lose ourselves for the Lord, we come to experience the truth of these words.

To be immersed in the Truth, in Christ—part of this process is prayer, in which we exercise our friendship with him and also come to know him: his way of being, of thinking, of acting. Praying is a journey in personal communion with Christ, setting before him our daily life, our successes and failures, our struggles and our joys—in a word, it is to stand in front of him. But if this is not to become a form of self-contemplation, it is important that we constantly learn to pray by praying with the Church. Celebrating the Eucharist means praying. We celebrate the Eucharist rightly if with our thoughts and our being we enter into the words which the Church sets before us. There we find the prayer of all generations, which accompany us along the way towards the Lord. As priests, in the Eucharistic celebration we are those who by their prayer blaze a trail for the prayer of today's Christians. If we are inwardly united to the words of prayer, if we let ourselves be guided and transformed by them, then the faithful will also enter into those words. And then all of us will become truly "one body, one spirit" in Christ.

To be immersed in God's truth and thus in his holiness—for us this also means to acknowledge that the truth makes demands, to stand up, in matters great and small, to the lie which in so many different ways is present in the world; accepting the struggles associated with the truth, because its inmost joy is present within us. Nor, when we talk about being sanctified in the truth, should we forget that in Jesus Christ truth and love are one. Being immersed in him means being immersed in his goodness, in true love. True love does not come cheap; it can also prove quite costly. It resists evil in order to bring men true good. If we become one with Christ, we learn to recognize him precisely in the suffering, in the poor, in the little ones of this world; then we become people who serve, who recognize our brothers and sisters in him, and in them, we encounter him.

"Sanctify them in truth"—this is the first part of what Jesus says. But then he adds: "I consecrate myself, so that they also may be consecrated in truth"—that is, truly consecrated (Jn 17:19). I think that this second part has a special meaning of its own. In the world's religions there are many different ritual means of "sanctification," of the consecration of a human person. Yet all these rites can remain something merely formal. Christ asks for his disciples the true sanctification which transforms their being, their very selves; he asks that it not remain a ritual formality, but that it make them truly the "property" of God himself. We could even say that Christ prayed on behalf of us for that sacrament which touches us in the depths of our being. But he also prayed that this interior transformation might be translated day by day in our lives; that in our everyday routine and our concrete daily lives we might be truly pervaded by the light of God.

On the eve of my priestly ordination, fifty-eight years ago, I opened the Sacred Scripture, because I wanted to receive once more a word from the Lord for that day and for my future journey as a priest. My gaze fell on this passage: "Sanctify them in the truth; your word is truth." Then I realized: the Lord is speaking about me, and he is speaking to me. This very same thing will be accomplished tomorrow in me. When all is said and done, we are not consecrated by rites, even though rites are necessary. The bath in which the Lord immerses us is himself—the Truth in person. Priestly ordination means: being immersed in him, immersed in the Truth. I belong in a new way to him and thus to others, "that his Kingdom may come." Dear friends, in this hour of the renewal of promises, we want to pray to the Lord to make us men of truth, men of love, men of God. Let us implore him to draw us ever anew into himself, so that we may become truly priests of the New Covenant. Amen.

Meditation

The priest is a consecrated man. Through the sacred act of Holy Ordination, the priest is introduced into a new kind of life, which removes him from worldly ties so that he can be given to God and united to Christ in an original, ineffable, irreversible bond. Indeed, through priestly ordination, the priest is marked on his very soul with a special character that identifies him with and configures and conforms him to Christ the Priest so as to make him capable of acting in the name of Christ the Head in person. This is what Vatican Council II affirms:

> By the sacrament of Order priests are configured to Christ the priest as servants of the Head, so that as co-workers with the episcopal order they may build up the Body of Christ, the Church. Like all Christians they have already received in the consecration of baptism the sign and gift of their great calling and grace. So they are enabled and obliged even in the midst of human weakness to seek perfection, according to the Lord's word: "You, therefore, must be perfect, as your heavenly Father is perfect" (Mt 5:48).
>
> But priests are bound by a special reason to acquire this perfection. They are consecrated to God in a new way in

their ordination and are made the living instruments of
Christ the eternal priest, and so are enabled to accomplish
throughout all time that wonderful work of his which with
supernatural efficacy restored the whole human race. Since
every priest in his own way assumed the person of Christ
he is endowed with a special grace. By this grace the priest,
through his service of the people committed to his care
and all the People of God, is able the better to pursue the
perfection of Christ, whose place he takes.[98]

"Certainly we [priests] are taken from among men and we
remain close to them. 'Christians with them,' as Saint Augustine
said. But we are 'set apart,' totally consecrated to the work of salvation to which the Lord Jesus calls us."[99]

You understand now how the priest becomes a man "*segregatus
in Evangelium Dei*: set apart for the Gospel of God" (Rom 1:1). He
no longer belongs to the world, or to himself, but rather is from
now on in a state that makes him the Lord's exclusive property.
The sacred character reaches such a depth that it integrally and
exclusively orients his whole being, to the point at which nothing
remains in him that he could dispose of, as though he were not a
priest of the Lord. Even when he performs actions that, by their
nature, are of a temporal order, the priest is still the minister of
God. In him, everything, absolutely everything, even what is profane,
must become "priestly," as in Jesus, Who was always a priest, always
acted as a priest, in all the manifestations of His life. Jesus identifies
us with Himself in such a way in the exercise of the powers that He
conferred on us that our personality disappears in the presence of

[98] *Presbyterorum ordinis* 12.
[99] John Paul II, Retreat for priests and seminarians in Ars, October
6, 1968.

His, since He is the one who acts through our intervention. Saint Josemaría Escrivá de Balaguer rightly said, "The sacrament of Orders, in effect, equips the priest to lend to our Lord his voice, his hands, his whole being. It is Jesus Christ who, in the Holy Mass, through the words of the consecration, changes the substance of the bread and wine into his Body, Soul, Blood, and Divinity."[100]

In the Sacrament of Penance, Jesus Himself pronounces the merciful, fatherly Word: "Your sins are forgiven" (Mt 9:2; Lk 5:20; 7:48; cf. Jn 20:23). He is the One Who speaks when the priest proclaims the Word of God, while carrying out his ministry in the name and in the spirit of the Church. Christ Himself cares for the sick, the children, and the sinners, when the pastoral love and solicitude of the sacred ministers accompanies them, watches over them, and protects them, as the shepherd protects his sheep from the wolves. You see: we find ourselves here at the pinnacle and the highest summit of Christ's priesthood, in which we are sharers, and which made the author of the Letter to the Hebrews exclaim: "About this we have much to say which is hard to explain" (Heb 5:11). Because he is consecrated to God, totally and exclusively dedicated to Him, the priest has no other good, wealth, patrimony, or treasure but God. So his heart can sing, day and night: "The LORD is my chosen portion and my cup; you hold my lot. The lines have fallen for me in pleasant places; yes, I have a goodly heritage. I bless the LORD who gives me counsel; in the night also my heart instructs me. I keep the LORD always before me; because he is at my right hand, I shall not be moved" (Ps 16:5-8).

We are not consecrated for our own sakes, but for God, for the Church and the world. This gift of the priesthood—remember

---

[100] See Josemaría Escrivá de Balaguer, Homily "A Priest Forever," April 13, 1973.

this always, beloved priests — is a miracle that has been performed in us, but not for us. It was performed for the Church, in other words, so that the world might be saved. The sacred dimension of the priesthood is ordered to its apostolic dimension — that is, to its mission, to pastoral ministry. "As the Father has sent me, even so I send you" (Jn 20:21). The Church is sent by God. She Herself does not take the initiative to go forth and travel through the world to give Her opinions and Her own judgment on human questions. She is sent to teach the Word and the laws of God. She does not go out from Herself in order to travel through the world proposing Her ideas or Her points of view concerning man and society, or Her moral opinions. The priest, too, therefore, is someone who has been sent. This is a new, essential connotation of priestly identity. Our priesthood is rooted in the missions of the Divine Persons, in their mutual gift at the heart of the Holy Trinity. Thus, our mission is a mission of salvation. "For God sent the Son into the world, not to condemn the world, but that the world might be saved through him" (Jn 3:17). Jesus preached the Good News of the Kingdom; He chose and formed His Apostles; He accomplished the work of redemption through His Cross and Resurrection; following the Apostles, we are associated in a special way with His work of salvation, so as to make it present, actual, and effective throughout the world. Saint John Mary Vianney went so far as to say: "Without the priest, the passion and death of Our Lord would be of no use. The priest is the one who continues the work of redemption on earth.... The priesthood is the love of the heart of Jesus."[101]

What we have to carry out, therefore, is not our work but, rather, the Father's plan, the Son's work of salvation. The Holy

---

[101] Nodet, *Jean-Marie Vianney.*

Spirit makes use of our spirits, our intellects, our mouths, our wills, our hands, and all our abilities so as to bring to fulfillment the work of salvation willed by the Holy Trinity. It is up to us especially to proclaim the Word constantly so as to evangelize, to express it in a way that will touch hearts and turn them resolutely toward Jesus Christ. We must proclaim clearly, boldly, and with fidelity the Word of God, without changing or diminishing it, without diluting or corrupting it.

It is a matter of performing again Jesus' act of offering at the Last Supper, of repeating His acts of forgiveness for sinners. Here it is a matter of helping sinners to acknowledge their sin, to encourage them to call it by its name. In the Gospel of Saint John, the scribes set a trap for Jesus by bringing an adulterous woman to him and saying to him: "Teacher, this woman has been caught in the act of adultery. Now in the law Moses commanded us to stone such. What do you say about her?" (Jn 8:4-5). Jesus, lowering His eyes, started to write with His finger on the ground. They insisted and demanded an answer to their question. He told them: " 'Let him who is without sin among you be the first to throw a stone at her.' And once more he bent down and wrote with his finger on the ground" (Jn 8:7-8). Then He stood up again and clearly reaffirmed the whole value and the unchangeable character of the divine laws and requirements; He showed how we should behave toward the sinner, whose human dignity He respects: "Neither do I condemn you; go, and do not sin again" (Jn 8:11). These are the words of the Gospel: evil is evil; sin is sin; adultery is adultery. But man is still called to holiness. He must continually make within himself the passage from the old man—that is, from the sinner to the New Man, who is born again by water and the Spirit (see Jn 3:5). We must denounce evil and invite sinners to conversion, to the radical abandonment of sin.

In putting on the person of Christ, we carry out in a certain way His mission and His office of mediator. We are the interpreters of the Word of God, the stewards of the divine mysteries (see 1 Cor 4:1; 2 Cor 6:4) to the people. We are sent to all His members: children, young people, the elderly, families, workers, the poor and the rich, the little and the great, the sick and the well, and especially those who are far from God, and the adversaries of the Church. No one is excluded from our pastoral charity. God excludes no one and shows preference for no one. He is the Father of all. "For he makes his sun rise on the evil and on the good, and sends rain on the just and on the unjust" (Mt 5:45). But He requires radical conversion and a return to Him by living in conformity with His laws. We priests are God's voice to invite people to conversion and to lead them to our Lord. We, too, on behalf of God, are fathers of everyone. We are their voices, praying and beseeching, exulting and groaning. We are their expiation (cf. 2 Cor 5:21).

We are in the midst of the world, sharing with the people of our time their anxieties, hopes, and joys and fighting alongside them for the coming of true freedom, justice, peace, and well-being for all. For, as Vatican Council II says again:

> The joy and hope, the grief and anguish of the men of our time, especially of those who are poor or afflicted in any way, are the joy and hope, the grief and anguish of the followers of Christ as well. Nothing that is genuinely human fails to find an echo in their hearts.[102]

However, priests must not let themselves be owned by the world or by the prince of this world, the Evil One (see Jn 17:14–15): "Do not be conformed," Saint Paul exhorts us, "to the opinions and

[102] *Gaudium et spes* 1.

tastes of this world" (see Rom 12:2). Work instead to align your personality, together with its aspirations, with God's will. Be signs of God. Understand, however, that the power of the sign lies not in conformity but in distinction. The light is distinguished from the darkness so as to be able to enlighten the path of the one who walks in the night and the darkness of our world. Salt contrasts with food so as to be able to give it its flavor. Fire is opposed to ice so as to be able to warm the limbs that have been numbed by the cold. Christ calls us the "light and salt of the world." In a scattered, confused world that has lost its bearings and is disoriented by the serious crises that we are going through at the moment—a crisis of faith, a crisis of the priesthood, anthropological and cultural crises, the desacralization of the liturgy—the power of the sign consists precisely in daring to be different. The sign must stand out all the more since apostolic activity requires great integration into the mass of humanity. We must dare to present ourselves distinctively as priests. We must dare to wear clothing that distinguishes us. We must dare to contrast with the spirit of the world. Without this, we will no longer be a sign of anything.

When we lose sight of these luminous perspectives, the figure of the priest becomes obscure; he experiences an identity crisis; his particular duties are no longer justified; his reason for being weakens. "A man for others": a priest surely is this, but by virtue of his particular way of being "a man for God." The service of God is the foundation on which he must construct his authentic service of men, which consists of freeing souls from the slavery of sin and leading mankind to the essential service of God. God, indeed, wants to make humanity a people that honors, glorifies, loves, and adores Him "in spirit and truth" (Jn 4:24).

The priest is not a social worker or the director of a nongovernmental organization who manages humanitarian assistance.

His service is not that of a physician, a politician, or a trade unionist.

The priest has an essential function to perform in the field of souls and their relationship with God. This is where he has to provide his assistance to the people of our time. Certainly, whenever circumstances require it, he will not neglect to offer material aid, too, by means of works of charity and the defense of justice. But as I already said, that is definitely a secondary service that must never cause us to lose sight of our principal service: to help souls discover the Father, to be open to Him, and to love Him above all else. This saying of the Apostles must be engraved deeply on the heart of every priest:

> It is not right that we should give up preaching the word of God to serve tables. Therefore, brethren, pick out from among you seven men of good repute, full of the Spirit and of wisdom, whom we may appoint to this duty. But we will devote ourselves to prayer and to the ministry of the word. (Acts 6:2-4)

Only in this way will the priest be assured of his identity. He will never feel useless or outmoded, even if he is forced to renounce all external activity. For if the essential elements of his priesthood remain—the Holy Sacrifice of the Mass, prayer, and penance—then he continues to render immense glory to God, as Christ did for thirty years, hidden in contemplation and attentive, interior, joyful listening to the will of the Father.

XII

Christ, the Perfect High Priest

Based on a meditation by Pope Francis

Introduction

The Letter to the Hebrews categorically affirms, as though in a splendid homily on Christ's Priesthood, that the only Priest is Christ. In reality, we have only one High Priest, and that is Jesus Christ. The priesthood of bishops and of priests is nothing but a sacramental participation in this unique priesthood which was accomplished in the only efficacious sacrifice: the one on the Cross.

> So also Christ did not exalt himself to be made a high priest, but was appointed by him who said to him, "You are my Son, today I have begotten you." ... In the days of his flesh, Jesus offered up prayers and supplications, with loud cries and tears, to him who was able to save him from death, and he was heard for his godly fear. Although he was a Son, he learned obedience through what he suffered; and being made perfect he became the source of eternal salvation to all who obey him, being designated by God a high priest according to the order of Melchizedek. (Heb 5:5, 7–10)

Let us explore this statement in greater depth by explaining the term "perfection," which is the outcome of Christ's offering. This will enable us to understand the nature of the new sacrifice and the orientation of the new priesthood, as Christ conceives of them.

In the Old Testament, priestly consecration was regarded as a separation that transported the priest into a separate domain and henceforth prohibited him from having any contact with the profane world. Deeply fascinated by his privileged relation with God, the Old Testament viewed the priest as a man absolutely dedicated to God, "a man for God," a man who was made to offer to God holy offerings and to send up a pleasing aroma of incense to Him. He must teach faithfully and transmit God's Word in its entirety. Because he belonged in this way to God, he had to break familial ties, as the Book of Deuteronomy emphasizes:

> [Levi] said of his father and mother, "I regard them not"; he disowned his brothers, and ignored his children. For they [the Levites] observed your word, and kept your covenant. They shall teach Jacob your ordinances, and Israel your law; they shall put incense before you, and whole burnt offering upon your altar. (Deut 33:9-10)

The priest also had authority to speak in God's name. He was His messenger. But a messenger is not always faithful; often he falsifies the Word of God. This still happens today when you heard priests presenting God in a vulgar, worldly way, and manipulating His Word as they please to adapt it to modern mentality and anti-Christian ideologies. The prophet Malachi says:

> For the lips of a priest should guard knowledge, and men should seek instruction from his mouth, for he is the

messenger of the LORD of hosts. But you have turned aside from the way, you have caused many to stumble by your instruction; you have corrupted the covenant of Levi, says the LORD of hosts. (Mal 2:7-8)

Furthermore, the Old Testament priest was pitilessly severe with sinners (Ex 32:26-29; Num 25:6-12).

Certainly, the priest remains and will remain the messenger of God; he will transmit to the people the teachings of God, His customs and laws, and not his own personal opinions. He will always make prayer rise to God like incense and will always place the whole burnt offering on the altar of God. But Christ will radically modify the perspective and this concept of priestly consecration. Indeed, the author of the Letter to the Hebrews, in meditating on the Passion and on the actual situation of Christ beside the Father, understood that sanctification by ritual separation, as the Old Testament conceived of it, was seriously deficient. In reality, it was not a genuine consecration, because it did not transform substantially and in depth the man who received it and therefore did not draw him closer to God. It was carried out by means of animal sacrifices (Lev 8; 9). Now, how could animal sacrifices bring perfection to a sullied human conscience or to a man who had been seriously, deeply corrupted by money, power, and human pleasures? Indeed, the blood of bulls and of goats is powerless to take away sins and to transform a man interiorly (see Heb 10:4). This is why, upon entering into the world, Christ said:

Sacrifices and offerings you have not desired, but a body have you prepared for me; in burnt offerings and sin offerings you have taken no pleasure. Then I said, "Behold, I have come to do your will, O God." (Heb 10:5-7)

The Passion of Christ was an act of priestly mediation that opened up for us a new, living path inaugurated especially for us through the veil—that is, the flesh of Christ. Jesus Christ is the true High Priest, established as the Head over the House of God (Heb 10:21). Thus, He gives us access to God, our heart cleansed of what sullies our conscience and our body washed with pure water. The secret of this act of mediation was the perfect union of two kinds of fidelity in Christ's heart: fidelity to God in filial obedience to the divine will and fidelity to human beings in fraternal solidarity.

Before Christ, people did worry, of course, about the holiness of priests, but only an external holiness could be provided (Heb 9:13); minutely prescribed rituals (oblations, anointings, special vestments) separated priests materially from the profane world and consecrated them symbolically to God. Their concern about making themselves pleasing to God and worthy of Him was expressed in this way. But what can ceremonies do, what can purely ritual and essentially external actions do, what can sacred vestments do, if man's heart remains sullied and profoundly ruined by sin? In his innermost depths, the priest must really be in agreement with God.

This radical requirement finds its complete fulfillment in Jesus Christ, and in Him alone. Christ's holiness has nothing to do with a ceremonial vestment designed to mask the priest's moral woes and personal unworthiness. Christ's holiness is an interior holiness that springs up in Him as the very source of His being, fills Him entirely, and spreads out around Him with an impetuous force. He can sanctify the people by His own blood (Heb 13:12; 9:14). This is the holiness of the only-begotten Son, Who obeys perfectly the will of God, His Father (Heb 10:7), Whom the Father can designate as the "beloved Son, with whom [he is] well pleased" (see Mk 1:11). And to prevent any misunderstanding, the author of the Letter to the Hebrews adds two epithets that rule out evil and the stain of sin. The perfect High Priest is innocent and immaculate. His innocence recalls what had already been said about Jesus: "For we have not a high priest who is unable to sympathize with our weaknesses, but one who in every respect has been tempted as we are, yet without sinning" (Heb 4:15). Sacrifice, in the strict sense of the term, is always a divine action, and not a human work. It is a transforming intervention by God. Man can present something to God, but it is impossible for him to sanctify what he brings. God alone, the source of all holiness, is capable of sanctifying the offering and of making it a sacrifice. The Old Testament understood this aspect of the situation perfectly. This is why it emphasized the role of fire from Heaven in carrying out sacrifices (Judg 6:19–23). We have in mind Elijah and the sacrifice on Mount Carmel (1 Kings 18:36–39).

Thus, priestly worship was conducted by means of a flame that had sprung up in the presence of Yahweh and consumed the victims offered on the altar (Lev 9:24). The sacred fire had then been maintained continually on the altar (Lev 6:12–13).

The author of the Letter to the Hebrews goes on to examine this insight in greater depth and to show how it is fulfilled in the Passion of Christ. It is no longer by means of a material flame that Christ offered Himself as a sacrifice but, rather, thanks to the eternal Spirit (Heb 9:14). The true divine fire, indeed, is none other than the Holy Spirit, Who alone is capable of bringing about the authentic sacrificial transformation. This is exactly what we ask at the Epiclesis during the Sacrifice of the Mass. When the priest asks for the Holy Spirit to be sent for the purpose of the consecration, he says: "Therefore, O Lord, we humbly implore you: by the same Spirit graciously make holy these gifts we have brought to you for consecration, that they may become the Body and + Blood of your

Son our Lord Jesus Christ, at whose command we celebrate these mysteries."[103] We ask for the outpouring of the power of the Holy Spirit on the offerings. Indeed, He was the one who brought about the Incarnation in the womb of the Virgin Mary; He was the one who descended in the form of a dove upon Jesus at His Baptism in the Jordan (Mt 3:16). Again, it was the Holy Spirit Who led Him into the wilderness to be tempted by Satan (see Mt 4:1). It is therefore important and indispensable to ask Him to produce the presence of Jesus under the appearances of the Eucharistic bread and wine. We invoke Him to come and sanctify and consecrate them, so that they might become the Body and Blood of Jesus Christ, our Lord. And after the Consecration, we invoke Him again so that He might make of us an eternal offering to the glory of God. Without the eternal Spirit, what are we capable of doing? Absolutely nothing. He is the One Who inspires in us the most complete obedience to the loving plan of God the Father, as well as complete solidarity among us, by forming one body and one spirit in Christ. The fire from Heaven that the earlier biblical traditions spoke about merely symbolized this.

The mention of Christ's sacrifice in the Letter to the Hebrews reminds us of Jesus' most tragic hour, in the Garden of Olives, and recalls these moments of agony at the prospect of His Passion and imminent death. At this hour of great suffering and loneliness, He prayed to the One Who could save Him from death and implored Him: "My Father, if it be possible, let this chalice pass from me; nevertheless, not as I will, but as you will" (Mt 26:39). His prayer, however, is thoroughly imbued with "godly fear" (Heb 5:7). This deep respect won for Him an answer to His prayers, but only through a sorrowful apprenticeship in obedience: "He learned

---

[103] Eucharistic Prayer III.

obedience through what he suffered" (Heb 5:8). His prayer and supplications were insistent: "Again, for the second time, he went away and prayed, 'My Father, if this [chalice] cannot pass unless I drink it, your will be done'" (Mt 26:42).

Saint Paul, for his part, emphasizes that Jesus divested Himself of what He was, in an act of freedom and love. He renounced the exercise of a privilege of glory that He had received from the Father before the beginning of the world, without thereby renouncing His divinity. Indeed, Christ moved from His condition as God to the condition of a slave in order to become similar to man. Father Albert Vanhoye comments:

> The most astounding point of the mystery of the Incarnation is precisely this: Christ assumed a nature like ours, a flesh like sinful flesh (cf. Rom 8:3), a human nature that needed to be transformed radically in order to be able to enter into God's heavenly intimacy. The deformation caused by disobedience had to be corrected by a superabundance of obedience. The preacher does not hesitate to say that Christ "learned obedience through what he suffered" (Heb 5:8). How can this disconcerting statement be understood? Did Christ therefore fail to be docile, even for a moment? Certainly not! He never sinned (cf. Heb 4:15; Jn 8:46; 1 Pet 1:19). From the beginning of his earthly life, he was guided by a perfect docility to the will of God (Heb 10:5–9). But there is good reason to make a distinction between a disposition to docility in principle and, on the other hand, the result in the human being achieved by an effective docility through sufferings and death.
>
> Just think: Docility to God can imbue all the fibers of our human nature only through the trials of life. This is why

suffering accepted and offered up with joy and serenity is a great school, a teacher, and at the same time a demonstration of the Love that we have for God. Christ accepted this painful requirement. We should add that his obedience was superabundant, because in complying with his Father's loving plan, he subjected himself to a fate that he did not deserve at all, a tragically unjust fate, that of an innocent man numbered among the worst criminals and sentenced to an ignominious execution (cf. Lk 22:37; 1 Pet 2:22–4). This is how Christ was consecrated High Priest. It is impossible to imagine closer solidarity with human misery. The crucified Christ was truly filled with weakness (Heb 5:2; cf. 2 Cor 13:4). Because of this, his priestly mediation is capable of reaching all human beings, even the most unfortunate and the most sinful. He won perfection by the way in which he confronted his sufferings and death, and he won it for our human nature. He can therefore communicate it to all who adhere to Him.[104]

Jesus does not insist on being treated as a divine person. He thus reveals the depths of His humiliation and self-denial. Of His divine status He keeps only the bond that unites Him to God in love, His being the Son: therefore He did not acquire the right of being God's equal in the Incarnation or even in His death on the Cross. He has always been that. The reason He puts on our humanity and is fully man is His love for the Father and His love for mankind.

In His Incarnation, His divine status does not appear as we imagine it, or rather, it appears as it is in the humility of the One

[104] É. Cothenet, M. Morgen, and A. Vanhoye, *Les Dernières Épîtres: Hébreux, Jacques, Pierre, Jean, Jude* (Paris: Bayard, 1977).

Who is capable of loving to the point of self-denial. Christ prefers others — that is, human beings — even if this preference proves painful and costly, because of the preference that He has for the Father, Who also wants to give Himself to us through Him and in Him.

The lowest point of this humiliation was reached in His death on the Cross. "He humbled himself and became obedient unto death, even death on a cross" (Phil 2:8). Humility becomes humiliation. It leads Christ to accept this type of death: a punishment for slaves in the Greco-Roman world and a symbol of a curse for the Jewish world. The Cross is therefore the abyss of self-emptying and, at the same time, the supreme expression and the summit of love. What is made explicit here is not His death "for us" but, rather, the supreme form assumed by the *kenosis* of the Son of God. Christ has given Himself up to the Father so much that He must go even to the Cross to express the abyss of love that He has for the Father and for us human beings. Christ's abasement is therefore not merely the active expression of obedience and humility. It is an act of self-denial through which the Son experiences and shows that He gives Himself up entirely to the Father and to mankind, and that, in Him and through Him, the Father reveals how much He gives Himself to us.

Thus, Christ's suppliant offering was accepted. His prayer, supplications, and tears obtained the sacrificial transformation wrought by the Spirit of God. This transformation took place through suffering and death. The event of Christ's Passion is therefore presented as a priestly offering. Intense prayer, presented to God with profound respect, is simultaneously a request and an offering. Indeed, the one who prays offers himself to God so that his prayer might be answered. He allows God to intervene concretely in his real life and to transform his being profoundly and radically. Moreover, the one who prays calls with all his heart for

God's divine intervention and aspires to this transformation from the depths of his being. Christ, who offered Himself in prayer to God's action and received it obediently was "made perfect" and at the same time consecrated High Priest.

We truly become priests only by carrying each day the cross of our fidelity to our priestly commitments. We become priests only by dying each day with Christ. There is no genuine priesthood without a cross.

Thus, during His Passion, Christ sealed with His own blood His solidarity with human beings. He loved them to the end and delivered Himself up for them, offering Himself to God as a sweet-smelling sacrifice (cf. Jn 13:1; Eph 5:2). At the conclusion of His Passion, Jesus is their brother more than ever. He made Himself like them in all things. "For he who sanctifies and those who are sanctified have all one origin. That is why he is not ashamed to call them brethren" (Heb 2:11). He is capable of understanding and helping them (Heb 4:15-16). But we should not forget to add that He made Himself like us in everything except sin. We must therefore oppose the illusion of those who might think that complicity in evil—under the pretext of an attitude of mercy and understanding or of pastoral accompaniment—is necessary in order to have complete solidarity with sinners. The contrary is true. Far from being a factor in authentic solidarity or welcome, complicity in evil only undermines solidarity, and trivializing or minimizing serious sins increases their ravages in the world.

What gives the Passion of Christ all its fruitfulness is obviously the perfection of love with which He confronted it, without ever yielding to a bad impulse (Heb 9:14; 1 Pet 2:21-25). The Passion of Christ brought His relation with men and His relation with God to their perfection. With all His might, Jesus turned to God and implored from Him a decisive intervention, and He persevered to the end in obeying God's will (Heb 5:8; 10:9). At the outcome of His Passion, He was Son of God more than ever. Indeed, His filial relation to the Father filled His transformed humanity with new life. What had previously been the "form of a servant" (Phil 2:7) and "the likeness of sinful flesh" (Rom 8:3) became the glorified body of Christ, "designated Son of God in power according to the Spirit of holiness by his resurrection from the dead" (Rom 1:4).

What is remarkable in this twofold aspect of Christ's consecration is that the two relations—with man and with God—are interdependent, or better, were founded on one another and became inseparable. We often think that we can draw near to God only by detaching ourselves completely from human beings, who are so unworthy of attention, or that someone who wants to accomplish an important work for the benefit of mankind is, by that very fact, in opposition to God, as though it obliged him to put God in parentheses. The existence of Jesus proves these two illusions false. Indeed, His perfect docility to the Father is what led Jesus to become the liberator of mankind (Heb 2:10-18; 5:7-10). Merciful Love, which drove Him to make the total gift of Himself in order to take away the sins of the world, has no other source than the heart of the Father. The priestly aspect of Christ's perfection is due precisely to the close union of the two relations in His risen humanity. Christ is the perfect priest because He has the ability to put us in communion with God and in communion with one another.

He does not do one without the other. He reveals to us the impossibility of separating the two dimensions of love, just as it is impossible to separate the divinity of Jesus from His humanity. This is what Saint John means in his First Letter: "If any one says, 'I love God,' and hates his brother, he is a liar; for he who does not love his brother whom he has seen, cannot love God whom he has not seen. And this commandment we have from him, that he who loves God should love his brother also" (1 Jn 4:20-21). To want the vertical dimension without the horizontal dimension is to doom oneself to failure. Similarly, to want the horizontal dimension without the vertical dimension of the relation with God is to try to cut off the river from its source or the tree from its roots. Only the union of the two dimensions is valid. We find it in the Cross of Jesus. Through the Cross, Christ attained His priestly perfection, which is a perfection of relation. The priest is a bridge that connects two banks: God and humanity.

Pope Francis: The Priestly Flesh of Christ

"Therefore, brethren, since we have confidence to enter the sanctuary by the blood of Jesus, by the new and living way which he opened for us through the curtain, that is, through his flesh, and since we have a great priest over the house of God, let us draw near with a true heart in full assurance of faith, with our hearts sprinkled clean from an evil conscience and our bodies washed with pure water. Let us hold fast the confession of our hope without wavering, for he who promised is faithful; and let us consider how to stir up one another to love and good works, not neglecting to meet together, as is the habit of some, but encouraging one another, and all the more as you see the Day drawing near.... But we are not of those who shrink back and are destroyed, but of those who have faith and keep their souls" (Heb 10:19-25, 39).

This text can serve as our introduction to the reflections that will accompany our prayer. It speaks about assurance, a sincere heart, the fullness of faith, unwavering hope, the impulse of charity. It tells us that this valor is due to the blood of Jesus, to his flesh. The week during which we celebrate the Passover of the Lord is most suitable context in which to contemplate the mysteries of his Passion and Resurrection, which are the mysteries of his outraged and glorified flesh. We defend ourselves from the disorder of sin, from the chaotic disintegration of our sinful conscience, by meeting as a family, as the nomadic tribes did in the desert before Israel: the chaos remains external. Easter saves us from the chaos. Within it is found the flesh of the Lamb that was "immolated" (Rev 5:9), who feeds us (Jn 6) and assures our courage and constancy, protecting us from cowardice, the fruit of the chaos of sin.

In his *Spiritual Exercises*, Saint Ignatius, while meditating on the mystery of the Passion, encourages us to ask for "grief, sorrow, and confusion because for my sins the Lord is going to the Passion" (SE 193), and also "It belongs to the Passion to ask for grief with Christ in grief, anguish with Christ in anguish, tears and interior pain at such great pain which Christ suffered for me" (SE 203). This leads us to consider "what Christ our Lord is suffering in His Humanity, or wants to suffer.... Here I will start to rally all the faculties of my soul and to force myself to grieve, be sad, and weep" (SE 195). And this also makes us reflect on the fact that "the Divinity hides Itself [during our Savior's Passion]; it could destroy its enemies and does not do it, and it abandons to the cruelest torments the most sacred Humanity which is united to it" (SE 196). Saint Ignatius, like Saint Thérèse, understands that the only sure way to reach the divinity is the most sacred humanity of Our Lord....

And in reflecting on the Passion, we must fathom this humanity: this man Jesus, who is God, yet suffers like a man, in his own body, in his own soul. And this is not a folktale, but real history, the only tangible path to follow, by which we must all pass in order to contemplate the Father, who reveals himself with the Son. We will contemplate the Passion in the flesh of Jesus, in our flesh. There is no other path if we truly want to profess that Jesus is alive, risen in his own flesh, with his open wounds and the transcendence of the Father's face. In contemplating the "Passion," we will contemplate the way in which the Lord demonstrated patience. We, his disciples, must understand what it means to suffer and to be patient, what that implies, so as to know him better and to love him better, so as to imitate him more closely.

God prepares his Son by making him "perfect through suffering" (Heb 2:10); he participates in flesh and blood so as to annihilate, through his death, the lord of death, that is, the devil, and to free those who, for fear of death, were subject to lifelong bondage (Heb 2:14ff.). "We see Jesus ... crowned with glory and honor because of the suffering of death, so that by the grace of God he might taste death for every one" (Heb 2:9). "Worthy are you to take the scroll and to open its seals, for you were slain and by your blood you ransomed men for God from every tribe and tongue and people and nation, and have made them a kingdom and priests to our God" (Rev 5:9-10). "Worthy is the Lamb who was slain, to receive power and wealth and wisdom and might and honor and glory and blessing" (Rev 5:12).

In order to save us, Jesus practices patience. I would like to emphasize some of the aspects of this "practice of patience," particularly its priestly dimension.

Thus, Jesus "practices patience" with his flesh, in his flesh. And through it, he is appointed a priest. "Therefore he had to be made like his brethren in every respect, so that he might become a merciful and faithful high priest in the service of God, to make expiation for the sins of the people. For because he himself has suffered and been tempted, he is able to help those who are tempted" (Heb 2:17-18). In his total dejection, in accepting his own failure, he offered one single sacrifice for sins (Heb 10:12), and he did not celebrate it with words, but with his flesh and blood:

> But when Christ appeared as a high priest of the good things that have come, then through the greater and more perfect tent (not made with hands, that is, not of this creation) he entered once for all into the Holy Place, taking not the blood of goats and calves but his own blood, thus securing an eternal redemption. For if the sprinkling of defiled persons with the blood of goats and bulls and with the ashes of a heifer sanctifies for the purification of the flesh, how much more shall the blood of Christ, who through the eternal Spirit of-fered himself without blemish to God, purify your conscience from dead works to serve the living God. (Heb 9:11-14)

> For it was fitting that we should have such a high priest, holy, blameless, unstained, separated from sinners, exalted above the heavens. He has no need,

> like those high priests, to offer sacrifices daily, first
> for his own sins and then for those of the people; he
> did this once for all when he offered up himself....
> [He is the] Son who has been made perfect for ever.
> (Heb 7:26-28)

We have drawn near to this priest, mediator of a new covenant, and to the purifying sprinkled blood that speaks more eloquently than Abel's.

Christ's priesthood is exercised in three phases: in the sacrifice of the Cross (in this sense it was "once for all"); presently (as intercessor with the Father; Heb 7:25); and at the end of time ("not to deal with sin but to save those who are eagerly waiting for him"; Heb 9:28), when Christ will commend all creation to the Father. During the second, current phase, Jesus Christ makes priestly intercession for us: "But he holds his priesthood permanently, because he continues for ever. Consequently he is able for all time to save those who draw near to God through him, since he always lives to make intercession for them" (Heb 7:24-25). Jesus Christ is alive, and he intercedes with his fullness of humanity and of divinity: "Since then we have a great high priest who has passed through the heavens, Jesus, the Son of God, let us hold fast our confession. For we have not a high priest who is unable to sympathize with our weaknesses, but one who in every respect has been tempted as we are, yet without sinning" (Heb 4:14-15). Through the mysteries of the Resurrection, Jesus, who was already established as Lord, shows his body, lets us touch his wounds, his flesh (Jn 20:20, 27; Lk 24:39-42). This body, these wounds, this flesh are intercession. Likewise, there is no other way to access the Father except this one. The

Father sees the Son's flesh and makes it attain salvation.... We find the Father in the wounds of Christ. Thus, he is alive in his glorious flesh, and he is alive in us.

To participate in his flesh, to practice patience with Him in His Passion so as to participate also in His glorification: this is the key concept of the Letter to the Hebrews: "We have an altar from which those who serve the tent have no right to eat" (Heb 13:10). This altar is Christ, his body hanging on the Cross.[105]

Meditation

Dear brother bishops and priests, since we have the privilege and the grace to share the priesthood of Christ, and since we aspire to be configured to Christ, let us be transformed by the flame of the Spirit of God. May He make us like His Son always. By communing in His sufferings, as Saint Paul says, may we become conformed to Him in His death.

And so, as Saint Gregory Nazianzen exhorts us:

We are not required to sacrifice young bulls or rams, beasts with horns and hoofs that are more dead than alive and devoid of feeling; but instead, let us join the choirs of angels in offering God upon his heavenly altar a sacrifice of praise.... I will say more: we must sacrifice ourselves to God, each day and in everything we do, accepting all that happens to us for the sake of the Word, imitating his passion by our

---

[105] Pape François, *Notre chair en prière*, translated from Spanish by Chrystèle Francillon (Paris: Parole et Silence, 2017).

sufferings, and honoring his blood by shedding our own. We must be ready to be crucified.

If you are a Simon of Cyrene, take up your cross and follow Christ. If you are crucified beside him like one of the thieves, now, like the good thief, acknowledge your God. For your sake, and because of your sin, Christ himself was regarded as a sinner; for his sake, therefore, you must cease to sin. Worship him who was hung upon the cross because of you, even if you are hanging there yourself. Derive some benefit from the very shame; purchase salvation with your death. Enter paradise with Jesus, and discover how far you have fallen. Contemplate the glories there, and leave the other scoffing thief to die outside in his blasphemy.

If you are a Joseph of Arimathea, go to the one who ordered his crucifixion, and ask for Christ's body. Make your own the expiation for the sins of the whole world. If you are a Nicodemus, like the man who worshiped God by night, bring spices and prepare Christ's body for burial. If you are one of the Marys, or Salome, or Joanna, weep in the early morning. Be the first to see the stone rolled back, and even the angels perhaps, and Jesus himself.[106]

At this point in our reflection, it is advisable to reemphasize something: the priests' identity is to prolong sacramentally the presence of the Good Shepherd in the midst of His flock. Then it becomes clear that each priest must be identified with the Good Shepherd not only by the sacramental character of his existence but also by his whole life. The temptation might be to imitate

[106] Saint Gregory Nazianzen, *Easter Homily*, in *Liturgy of the Hours*, 2:393.

the life of Jesus materially and to think that a priest must be first of all a traveling preacher, a miracle-worker, a spiritual director. Pope Francis, in this moving text, invites us, on the contrary, to a much more profound identification. He invites us not to "do" but to "suffer." Jesus is a priest by His Passion, by His ability to accept suffering and human failures heroically and to die for love of the truth. And to us has been given the favor not only of believing in Christ but also of suffering for Him (cf. Phil 1:29).

People often expect the priest to act, to take initiatives, to organize, to be a social leader and an excellent manager. They would like him to be the head of a company. Pope Francis invites us to change our way of looking at this. He recalls that being a priest consists, in the first place, of suffering, of bearing the consequences with Christ. Being a priest boils down to identifying with Christ's Passion and prolonging it every day. To be a priest is to say, as Saint Paul does: "I bear on my body the marks of Jesus" (Gal 6:17).

In a world centered solely on the material aspects of life and on technological, economic, and political success, what can God do, if not suffer, especially if man commits his own heart to deliberate, stubborn egotism? In a world of ingratitude, indifference, or even manifest hostility to God, in a society that constantly insults God by deliberately violating His laws, how could the priest shirk suffering? The priest is called to be nailed on the Cross with Christ, so he is no longer the one who lives, but rather Christ lives in him. Every time he celebrates the Mass, he commemorates the Sacrifice of Jesus on Golgotha. He renews it by the power of the Holy Spirit. And at that moment, he is, so to speak, seized by the power of the Holy Spirit, and the words that he pronounces possess the same efficacy as those that came forth from the mouth of Christ during the Last Supper. And in a profound desire for total identification with Christ, he must be able to say, as Saint Bernard did: "I am nailed to the Cross with Christ, my side against his side, my hands against his hands, my feet against his feet, the same nails piercing him and me, our blood mingling in one blood." Christ crucified is really present in each priest. I think, in particular, of priests who are sick or handicapped, confined to bed in the hospital or at home, thus filling up in their flesh what is lacking in the trials of Christ for His Body, which is the Church (cf. Col 1:24). And even if illness makes him incapable of celebrating Holy Mass, that is really the moment when he celebrates the Holy Sacrifice fully, by joyfully offering his sufferings and by mingling his trials and his agony with Christ's. His sickbed becomes the altar of Sacrifice.

But as we just emphasized by mentioning sick priests, we do not have to reduce the presence of the Passion to the ritual renewal of it. The whole life of a priest is a presence of the Passion, presence of the priestly, offered flesh of Christ the Priest, to repeat the words of Pope Francis. All of priestly life must have a sacrificial form, Saint John Paul II said. It is important, therefore, for us to renew profoundly our way of looking at the life of priests in this light. A sick, bedridden priest is not useless and ineffective; if he experiences the Passion in his flesh, he is fully and totally a priest. On the contrary, a restless priest who seeks only human success and the admiration of the worldly public runs a high risk of being useless. This does not mean that priests must renounce zeal and missionary inventiveness; quite the contrary! It tells us, rather, that every act of a priest, each one of his initiatives, must be done with a profound union to Jesus' Passion in his heart.

A priest must offer himself incessantly with Christ. Every time he implements a project, his heart should sing interiorly the words of Jesus: "Not what I will, but what You will." Thus, human success and failure are not his ultimate criteria in making a judgment. He does not act as the owner of his actions but offers them, while constantly ready to be dispossessed of what he does, what he has, and what he is.

As long as the People of God expect priests to be covered with human glory and social success, we have to expect abuses of authority, resounding falls, and, above all, a drift away from the priesthood of Christ and a lethal deformation of it. We should expect priests who are identified with Christ on the Cross. No one cheered Christ on the way to Golgotha; He was not applauded but, rather, was covered with spittle and insults. A priest who wins acclaim should worry; a popular priest should ask himself some fundamental questions. If preaching the Word of God does not lead us to the Passion, maybe it is because we are preaching too timidly, fearful of proclaiming Jesus Christ in full fidelity to the Word of God and to Tradition, or because we are overly concerned about pleasing and have compromised with the spirit of the world. As Saint John Paul II declares:

> According to Saint Paul, [to be a priest] means above all to be *a steward of the mysteries of God.* "This is how one should regard us, as servants of Christ and stewards of the mysteries of God. Now it is required of stewards that they be found trustworthy" (1 Cor 4:1-2). The word "steward" cannot be replaced by any other. It is deeply rooted in the Gospel; it brings to mind the parable of the faithful steward and the unfaithful one (cf. Lk 12:41-48). The steward is not the owner, but the one to whom the owner entrusts his goods so that he will manage them justly and responsible. In exactly the same way the priest receives from Christ the treasures of salvation, in order duly to distribute them among the people to whom he is sent.... No one may

consider himself the "owner" of these treasures; they are meant for us all. But, by reason of what Christ laid down, the priest has the task of administering them.[107]

Therefore, just as Jesus did not teach His own doctrine but taught that of the One Who sent Him, so, too, the priest must not seek worldly success or teach his opinions to please people but must teach only the Gospel and the teaching of Jesus Christ (cf. Jn 7:16-18).

Is it necessary, then, to seek failure? Certainly not. It is up to a priest to continue his formation, to study constantly, to be a *theodidactos*, a "pupil of God," to deepen his personal relationship with our Lord, to ask himself challenging questions, to improve himself so as to be more effective. But he must know interiorly that grace will never be the product of a technique, that it always flows from the open heart of Jesus on the Cross.

A priest whose heart is not broken and open may well master all the techniques of preaching and management, but his work will remain fruitless. Priests must be competent in theology, preaching, and methods of pastoral care, but their competence must be irrigated and animated by a life of grace, or else it will be sterile.

[107] Pope John Paul II, *Gift and Mystery*, 71-72.

XIII

Forming the Soul of a Priest

Based on a meditation by Pius XII

--------◆∞◆--------

Introduction

A great deal is at stake in the formation of priests. Above all, it is the responsibility of the diocesan bishop. Every bishop ought to have the freedom to open a genuine seminary for his diocese. I know that it is popular nowadays to call into question the classic model of the seminary. Sometimes formation programs at universities are favored. But is that advisable for a future priest? A seminarian is not just a student. He does not only have to accumulate philosophical and theological knowledge. A priest is not, in the first place, a professor but a minister of Christ. People do not expect him to be only a scholar. It is important for his soul, his thought, his whole being to be formed, molded by Christ the priest. In order for that to happen, it is necessary for him to experience a form of priestly life. This involves certain essential elements: a personal and communal prayer life, a form of retreat and distance from the world and from media agitation, a fraternal life of charity in obedience to the bishop or to his representative.

219

These elements outline what Hans Urs von Balthasar called a "Tridentine" seminary. We see too many seminaries that are merely houses for immature, solitary students. On the contrary, a seminary should be a place of apprenticeship in the fullness of priestly life. Now, that life is not characterized primarily by nervous, unbridled activism. Priestly life is primarily a life of intercession with Christ the Priest. In seminaries, the main element of formation is therefore the interior life. We ought to see liturgies celebrated carefully there. Daily Mass and the recitation of the Divine Office in common are structural elements in the formation of a priestly soul. The identity of a minister of Christ is forged at the foot of the altar and in the daily repetition of the psalms. By joining each day in the sacramental renewal of the sacrifice of the Cross on the altar, little by little the soul espouses the sentiments of Christ's priestly heart.

In order to enter fully into this spiritual path, so as to open his temperament and his whole nature to Christ, the seminarian will have to acquire the human equilibrium of the virtues. I remember very clearly the insistence of Monsignor Raymond-Marie Tchidimbo, then archbishop of Conakry-Guinea, about the human and spiritual qualities of candidates to the priesthood, and especially about their moral integrity and noble sentiments. Often he would come to pay us a visit at the minor seminary in Kindia. And I can still hear him thundering in the auditorium: "The first reason for dismissing a seminarian is duplicity. The second reason—duplicity, and the third—duplicity." His inflexible, forceful, and demanding language scared us, but he wanted to make it clear to us that a man called to the priesthood must be virile, upright, true, and a man of integrity. Monsignor Tchidimbo considered truth, fidelity, straightforwardness, and honesty to be indispensable virtues about which a bishop could not compromise. Before being a priest, it is necessary to be a man, seminary formators traditionally say.

Two main elements are conducive to acquiring this equilibrium of moral virtues. First, communal and fraternal life. In it, everyone learns to do his part in working for the common good. In it, one learns justice and mercy among brothers. In it, one practices forgiving offenses and truth in friendly relations. This moral manliness, this simplicity in virtue should enable seminarians to break with the image of the oversensitive, lazy, and emotionally immature cleric. A priest must be a balanced man. In order to be a priest with one's whole soul, one must first be capable of being a just, generous, balanced, and virile man. Many problems of emotional excesses and abuse would have been avoided if seminaries formed men in real emotional maturity, as experienced in friendship and fraternal sincerity. A major contribution to this is work done in common, including manual labor.

One sign of this maturity is the ability to obey sincerely and simply. Therefore, in the seminary, it must be possible to experience obedience to the bishop concretely. This presupposes that the bishop truly behaves as the father of the seminarians and of his priests. He ought to be able to live with them, pray with them, listen to them, and counsel them. What a joy to see a bishop surrounded by his seminarians like a father with his children! This is the way to develop the trust between the bishop and his priests that should last their whole lives. How many priests are too lonely! How many priests go through deep spiritual crises without the fatherly presence of their bishop! Episcopal fatherhood can no longer be an empty word reserved for liturgical texts. It must become a reality.

––––––––––––––––– ⬦∞⬦ –––––––––––––––––

Address of Pope Pius XII to the Seminarians in Les Pouilles[108] (excerpts)

Preparing for the priesthood means forming a priestly soul

The sacramental character of Holy Orders puts God's seal on an eternal covenant which is, so to speak, the manifestation of his love of predilection, which requires from the chosen creature a response of love that is expressed in holiness of life and complete adherence to the will of the Father. Concretely, a man becomes a priest if he forms for himself a priestly soul by continually engaging all his faculties and spiritual energies in the work of conforming his soul to Christ, the eternal High Priest. He is the model of the priest. The work of educating and forming seminarians must be essentially oriented toward this spiritual metamorphosis; its difficulties must not be concealed, and its interior joys must not be stifled.

The Priest Is, Above All, Christ's Minister

The seminarian will also acquire this sort of idea about his future activity as a "servant of Christ" and a "steward of the mysteries of God" (cf. 1 Cor 4:1), as a "fellow worker of God" (cf. 1 Cor 3:9). The sacred ministry will have to

[108] Pius XII had prepared an address for the occasion of the celebration of the fiftieth anniversary of the foundation of the regional seminary in Les Pouilles, France. The audience had been scheduled for Sunday, October 19, 1958. This lucid, spiritually profound, and exceptionally clear text was never presented, since Pope Pius XII died ten days before that date.

influence every one of his actions and works. He will be
a man with holy and upright intentions, like those that
prompt God to act. Any admixture of personal intention
coming from human nature alone should be considered
unworthy of its sacred character and as an evasion. If certain activities bring him plenty of human satisfaction, he
will be grateful to God for this, accepting it as a help, but
not a substitute, for his holy intentions. But his principal
action will be in the strict sense priestly, in other words, the
action of a mediator of men, by offering to God the sacrifice
of the New Testament, by dispensing the Sacraments and
the divine word, along with the recitation of the Divine
Office, in which he represents all humanity and prays for it.

Preparing for the Priesthood Means Becoming Instruments in God's Hands

God is immensely benevolent toward those whom he
chooses as instruments of his salvific will! As a trustee and
steward of the means of salvation, a priest cannot avail
himself of them by his own free will, because he is the
"servant" of them, yet he also keeps intact his personal
autonomy, the freedom of his acts, and his responsibility
for them. Consequently, he is a conscious instrument of
Christ, who, like an ingenious sculptor, makes use of him
as a chisel to model the divine image in souls. Woe to him
if the instrument refuses to follow the divine artist's hand;
woe to him if he deforms the design as he pleases! The
work would prove to be very mediocre if the instrument was
inept, through its own fault! The purpose of seminaries is
precisely this: to guide young seminarians so that they may
become perfect, effective, and docile instruments of Christ.

For Eternity

The Need for a Solid Theological Formation

Although the perfection and effectiveness of the instrument depend on God, docility depends on human will. An instrument that is not docile but rebellious in the artist's hands is useless and dangerous. It is instead an instrument of perdition. But God can do everything with a well-disposed instrument, even if it is imperfect. In contrast, he can do nothing with a rebellious instrument. Docility means obedience, and even more, "being at God's disposal" for any work whatsoever, for any need, for any change. True availability is attained through detachment from one's personal views, one's own interests, and even from the holiest enterprises. This detachment is founded on this humble truth taught by Our Lord: "When you have done all that is commanded you, say: 'We are unworthy servants!'" (Lk 17:10). As We already noted, this does not imply indifference toward the assigned work, nor the absence of all legitimate sense of satisfaction in seeing the results obtained. The discipline that is imposed on you in the seminary with an altogether fatherly affection has no other purpose than to educate you to remain perfectly docile to Christ and the Church.

Prepare for Perseverance

Everything seems easy, dear seminarians, in these years of preparation, of which you will cherish a fond memory and a bit of nostalgia. Your present enthusiasm, the upright intentions that inspire you, the impetus toward perfection that you seek: all this foretells a fruitful, tranquil priestly ministry, the serenity of which will be untroubled even by the battle against God's enemies. With all Our heart We wish you this; but We must not remain silent about the reality. Until now you have been prepared to suffer everyday difficulties by practicing the virtues of vigilance and perseverance. But as the years pass, and your weariness and the battles increase, and your physical and psychological strength naturally decreases, it is quite normal if your soul happens to go through a profound crisis that seems to submerge every ideal and to extinguish even the most ardent zeal. In such crises, which are sometimes accompanied by the unexpected unleashing of the passions, we must recognize forgetfulness of the most elementary prudence and sometimes forgetfulness of the most imperative duties. But sometimes, too—and not infrequently—the crisis arrives like an unexpected typhoon on a calm sea. The feverish rhythm of modern life which keeps the mind from reflecting, the thousand snares met along the way each day, the contact with more or less consciously troubled minds—all this works together to create interior difficulties....

We encourage you, dear seminarians, to train now for such a possibility by foreseeing it and preparing for it. Above all, gauge your strength, but including in the one sum total the strength that God will give you; and do everything possible to keep it intact and increase it, by adopting the precautions and the resources that are plentifully offered by the Church. In practicing perseverance, you must rely on the wise guidance of spiritual directors and, furthermore, on the uninterrupted correction of your morals, on the orderliness of your daily routine, on moderation in undertaking and carrying out external activities. God is calling you to a sublime dignity, and many immediate salutary aids are available to you; but it could all end in sorrowful disappointment unless you apply yourself, like the wise virgins, to watching and persevering. To the elderly clergy We wish to recommend: do not discourage the young priest. No doubt disappointments are inevitable, whether they result from general human conditions, or from particular local reasons; but they must not result from the fact that older priests, who perhaps have been discouraged by the disappointments of real life, dull the lively energies of the young clergy. When mature experience does not demand a resolute No, let him plan projects, let him try, and if nothing succeeds, comfort him and encourage him to try new endeavors.

Meditation

Every time we read the Gospel, we observe that Jesus always entrusted a responsibility to a person, never to an institution. The Church is founded on the person of the bishop and not on the bishops' conference or diocesan chanceries. There is nothing more grotesque than to think that Christ had intended to create committees! It is advisable to teach seminarians to assume their responsibilities fully. They must rediscover a Catholic truth: in the Church, everything is personal; nothing should be anonymous. However, many bishops and priests today do hide behind anonymous structures, such as bishops' conferences, committees, or even synodal ways. All these committees and subcommittees, these groups and these offices of every sort are sometimes useful, but they must not stifle and annihilate the personal responsibility of the bishop and make him disappear behind structures that guide and make decisions in his name. Everyone complains about the priest shortage, and it is true, while thousands of clergymen are put in charge of a bureaucracy that runs the risk of killing the missionary drive of the Church. What good are all these learned documents, these papers that no one reads and that have no importance anyway for the Christian people and the living Church? Faith is much simpler than all that. Jesus wants real, free persons who are fully responsible for their acts and are autonomous, docile instruments in His hands—not structures or machines.

Indeed, as Pius XII recalls: "As a trustee and steward of the means of salvation, a priest cannot avail himself of them by his own free will, because he is the 'servant' of them, yet he also keeps intact his personal autonomy, the freedom of his acts, and his responsibility for them. Consequently he is a conscious instrument of Christ, who, like an ingenious sculptor, makes use of him as a chisel to model the divine image in souls." This is why Pius XII insists on the role of the seminaries: "The purpose of seminaries is precisely this: to guide the young seminarians so that they may become perfect, effective, and docile instruments," men who feed on and live by prayer, constantly prostrate before the tabernacle, persons perfectly aware of what an extraordinary gift it is to share in Christ's priesthood.

The sacred power to act *in persona Christi* in the Church—in other words, like Christ, the Head of the Church in person—has always had a personal character. It is the peculiar effect of the Sacrament of Holy Orders to modify substantially the supernatural organism of the ordinand, in such a way that while acting by his own movement, he becomes the instrumental cause of Christ's priestly action. As a living instrument of Christ, the priest gathers into the communion of the Church those whom Jesus saved for eternity by His one sacrifice, and he does this by voluntarily lending his own person, forever and every day, to Jesus, the one High Priest.

For Eternity

To be another Christ or Christ Himself for every human person is what we call being an "apostle." To be an apostle is to tend to be configured to Christ and to resemble Him. And to resemble Christ is to tend toward perfection. In other words, it means to work to acquire the qualities needed to carry out the priestly ministry. We can say that this is also the requirement of the Christian people. For they want to recognize in their pastor not only a man who is distinguished by his gifts and virtues, including natural ones, but also a person who is prudent and balanced in his judgments, sure and calm in his actions, impartial and orderly, generous and ready to forgive, a friend of harmony and peace and an enemy of laziness. For the priest, even the so-called natural virtues are requirements for the apostolate because, without them, he would offend or repel others by his lack of respect and consideration.

John Paul II, in his Post-Synodal Apostolic Exhortation *Pastores dabo vobis* echoes Pope Pius XII when he insists on human and philosophical formation as the foundation of all priestly formation. He places the accent on spiritual formation, in communion with God and in search of Christ. He dwells at length on intellectual and theological formation for an understanding of the faith and on pastoral formation so as to live and transmit the charity of Jesus Christ, the Good Shepherd.[109]

To this perfection that is already acquired, as much as it is possible to do so, we must add the perfections proper to the priestly state—namely, holiness. In his address, Pius XII insists that sanctity is necessary for a priest. He must be aware that God is constantly calling him to sanctity because he is the very presence, the prolongation, of Jesus Christ on Earth.

[109] See John Paul II, Post-Synodal Apostolic Exhortation *Pastores dabo vobis* (March 25, 1992), nos. 42–59.

XIV

Son of the Church

Based on a meditation by Saint Augustine

Introduction

Saint Gregory the Great speculated that the Church at the time of Christ was in Her infancy and therefore did not yet perform Her maternal function. She was very little then, a newborn, and could not preach the Word of Life. But after receiving the Holy Spirit, She became a fertile mother, and that is when salvation spread through the entire world, thanks to the ministry of preachers and pastors. The Church is called "adult" when, in union with the Word of God and filled with the Holy Spirit, She is enriched by the children whom She conceives and bears. She brings them into the world by converting them and making them true believers, true disciples of Jesus Christ. And Benedict XVI says that a genuine son of the Church does not attach too much importance to the struggle to reorganize the external forms of the Church:

> Those who really believe ... live on what the Church always is; and if one wants to know what the Church really is one must go to them. For the Church is most present,

not where organizing, reforming, and governing are going on, but in those who simply believe and receive from her the gift of faith that is life to them. Only someone who has experienced how, regardless of changes in her ministers and forms, the Church raises men up, gives them a home and a hope, a home that is hope—the path to eternal life—only someone who has experienced this knows what the Church is, both in days gone by and now.[110]

As I already put it in an earlier book:

What we urgently need is to start looking again at everything with the eyes of faith. By reforming institutions non-stop, you maintain the illusion that the important thing is what we are doing, our human action, which we regard as the only effective measure. This type of reform therefore only shifts the problem. I think that it is essential and urgent to discern the true nature of the crisis [that we are going through right now] and to realize that the evil is not found solely in the ecclesial institutions. Minor modifications made to the organization of the Curia cannot rectify mind-sets, feelings, and morals. What is a "reform" in the profound meaning of the term? It is about a reformation. A return to the pure form, the one that comes from God's hands. The true reform of the Church consists of allowing ourselves to be shaped by God once again. In *The Ratzinger Report* [p. 53], Cardinal Ratzinger declared:

Hence, true "reform" does not mean to take great pains to erect new façades (contrary to what certain ecclesiologies

---

[110] Joseph Ratzinger, *Introduction to Christianity*, trans. J.R. Foster, revised ed. (San Francisco: Ignatius Press, 2004), 343–344.

think). Real "reform" is to strive to let what is ours disappear as much as possible so [that] what belongs to Christ may become more visible. It is a truth well known to the saints. Saints, in fact, reformed the Church in depth, not by working up plans for new structures, but by reforming themselves. What the Church needs in order to respond to the needs of man in every age is holiness, not management.[111]

Saint Augustine, Letter 208

I do not doubt that your mind has been troubled because of your own faith and the weakness or wickedness of others, although the Apostle, filled with the marrow of charity, confesses and says: "Who is weak and I am not weak? Who is scandalized and I am not on fire?" [2 Cor 11:29]. For this reason, being distressed and anxious for your salvation which is in Christ, I have thought it advisable to send your Holiness this letter of consolation or exhortation, since you have become very close to me in the body of our Lord Jesus Christ which is His Church and the unity of His members; you are loved as an honorable member in His body, and you live with us by His Holy Spirit.

Hence, I advise you not to be too deeply disturbed by these scandals, because their coming was foretold so that, when they came, we might remember that they had been

---

[111] Robert Cardinal Sarah and Nicolas Diat, *The Day Is Now Far Spent*, trans. Michael J. Miller (San Francisco: Ignatius Press, 2019), 108–109.

foretold and might not be greatly troubled by them. The
Lord Himself thus foretold them in the Gospel: "Woe to
the world because of scandals! For it must needs be that
scandals come, but nevertheless woe to that man by whom
the scandal cometh" [Mt 18:7; Lk 17:1]. And who are
those men if not those of whom the Apostle says: "seeking
the things that are their own, not the things that are Jesus
Christ's" [Phil 2:21]? Therefore, there are some who occupy
the pastoral chair in order to care for the flock of Christ,
but there are others who sit in it to gratify themselves by
temporal honors and worldly advantages. These are the
two kinds of pastors, some dying, some being born, who
must needs continue in the Catholic Church itself until
the end of the world and the judgment of the Lord. If there
were such men in the times of the Apostles, whom the
Apostle lamented as false brethren when he said: "Perils
from false brethren" [2 Cor 11:26], yet whom he did not
proudly dismiss but bore with them and tolerated them,
how much more likely is it that there should be such men
in our times, when the Lord speaks openly of this time of
the world which is nearing its end, saying: "Because iniquity
hath abounded the charity of many shall grow cold!" But
what follows ought to console and encourage us: "He that
shall persevere to the end," He says, "he shall be saved" [Mt
24:12-13; 10:22; Mk 13:13].

Now, as there are good and bad shepherds, so also
among the flocks there are good and bad. The good are
signified by the name of sheep, while the bad are called
goats. But they feed, mingled equally together, until "the
prince of pastors shall appear" [1 Pet 5:4], who is called
the "one shepherd" [Jn 10:16], who, as He promised, shall

"separate them as the shepherd separateth the sheep from the goats" [Mt 25:32]. He has commanded us to gather them together, but for Himself He has reserved the task of separating them, because He who cannot err is the one who ought to separate. As to these proud servants who have lightly dared to separate before the time which the Lord has reserved for Himself, they ought rather to be separated themselves from Catholic unity, for how can those who are tainted with schism have an untainted flock?

Our Shepherd urges us, then, to remain in unity; not to abandon the Lord's threshing floor because we are offended by the scandals of chaff; but rather, as good grain, to persevere to the end, to the time of winnowing, and by the strong weight of our charity to bear with the lightness of the straw. In the Gospel He speaks to us of good shepherds [Jn 10:11, 14], and tells us not to place our hope even in them because of their good works, but to glorify the "Father who is in heaven" [Mt 5:16] who made them such; and He speaks of bad shepherds whom He wished to signify by the name of Scribes and Pharisees, whose teaching is good, but whose conduct is bad [Mt 23:2-3].

Of the good shepherds He speaks thus: "You are the light of the world. A city seated on a mountain cannot be hid; neither do men light a candle and put it under a bushel, but upon a candlestick, that it may shine to all that are in the house. So let your light shine before men that they may see your good works and glorify your Father who is in heaven" [Mt 5:14-16]. But He warns the sheep against bad shepherds by saying: "They have sitten on the chair of Moses, whatsoever they shall say to you do ye, but according to their works do ye not; for they say and do not" [Mt 23:2-3]. In hearing them, the sheep of Christ hear His voice even through bad teachers, and they do not forsake His unity, because the good which they hear them say is not theirs but His; therefore, the sheep feed in safety, because even under bad shepherds they are nourished in the Lord's pasture. But they do not do the deeds of the bad shepherds, because such works are not His but theirs. On the other hand, those who follow good shepherds not only hear the good things which they say, but also imitate the good deeds which they do. Of such was the Apostle who said: "Be ye followers of me as I also am of Christ" [1 Cor 11:1; 4:16]. That light was enkindled from the eternal light, the Lord Jesus Christ Himself, and was put upon a candlestick because he gloried in Christ's cross. Thus he said: "But God forbid that I should glory save in the cross of our Lord Jesus Christ" [Gal 6:14]. And as he did not seek the "things that were his own, but the things that were Jesus Christ's" [Phil 2:21], although he exhorted those whom he had begotten by the Gospel [1 Cor 4:15] to imitate him, he severely upbraided those who made a schism out of the names of Apostles, and rebuked those who said: "I am of Paul." "Was Paul crucified for you?" he said, "or were you baptized in the name of Paul?" [1 Cor 1:12-13]

Hence we understand that good shepherds seek not their own, but the things that are of Jesus Christ, and that, while good sheep imitate the deeds of good shepherds, they do not place their hope in those by whose ministry they have been gathered together, but rather in the Lord by whose Blood they have been redeemed. Thus, when they happen to meet bad shepherds, who preach Christ's doctrine but do their own bad works, they do what these say but they do not do what these do, and they do not forsake the pastures of unity because of the sons of iniquity. There are both good and bad in the Catholic Church, which has spread not in Africa alone, as the Donatist sect has done, but through all nations, as it was promised, and which extends throughout the whole world, as the Apostle says, bringing forth fruit and increasing [Col 1:6]. Those who are separated from it cannot be good as long as they hold views contrary to it; even if an apparently laudable conduct seems to point out some of them as good, the very division makes them bad, according to the Lord's words: "He that is not with me is against me, and he that gathereth not with me scattereth" [Mt 12:30].

Therefore, I urge you, lady deservedly cherished and daughter honored among the members of Christ, to hold faithfully to what the Lord has bestowed on you, and to love Him and His Church with your whole heart [Mt 22:37], because He has not allowed you to lose the fruit of your virginity or to perish among the lost. For, if you were to go out of this world separated from the unity of Christ's Body, it would profit you nothing to have preserved the integrity of your own body. But God, "who is rich in mercy" [Eph 2:4], has dealt with you according to the words of the Gospel. When the guests invited to the supper of the householder made excuses, among other things he said: "Go out into the highways and hedges, and as many as you shall find, compel them to come in" [Lk 14:18, 23]. Consequently, although you owe a most sincere affection to His good servants through whose agency you were forced to come in, you should place your hope in Him who prepared the banquet, by whom you are also invited to an eternal and blessed life. By confiding your heart to Him, then, as well as your purpose, your holy virginity, your faith, your hope, and your charity, you will not be troubled by the scandals which will abound until the end, but you will be saved by the unshaken strength of your devotion and by your perseverance to the end in the Lord and in His glorious unity. Let me know in your answer how you have felt about my anxiety for you, which I have tried, as best I could, to express in my letter. May the mercy and grace of God guard you.[112]

Meditation

The Church produces men and women of faith, true believers, and saints. She brings into the world true witnesses of Christ who go so far as to die for Him and for the sake of the Gospel. She produces sons and daughters of God. Saint Augustine had already described this mystery of the *Mater Ecclesia* magnificently in a letter:

> Mother Church is also the mother of your mother. She has conceived both of you from Christ; she has been in travail for you with the blood of martyrs; she has given birth to you into everlasting light; she has fed and feeds you with the milk of faith, and, though she prepares more solid foods, she sees with horror that you want to wail like small children without teeth. This mother, spread throughout the whole world, is troubled by such varied and multiple attacks

---

[112] Augustine of Hippo *Letters*, vol. 5 of Fathers of the Church (Washington, DC: Catholic University of America Press, 1956), 24–28.

from errors that her aborted offspring now do not hesitate to war against her with unrestrained arms. Because of the neglect and laziness of certain ones whom she holds on her lap, she grieves that her members become cold in many places and become less able to embrace the small children. From where but from other children, from other members, in whose number you are included, does she demand the help that is due her in justice? Are you going to neglect her needs and turn to the words that the flesh speaks? Does she not strike the ears with more serious complaints? Does she not have a womb that is more precious and breasts filled with heavenly food?[113]

As early as the fourth century, at the time of Saint Augustine, until the sixth century, in the midst of the disorder and confusion caused in the East by all sorts of dramatic events, little by little the bishops found themselves vested with some political authority, and these new responsibilities often distracted them from their pastoral ministry and their specifically spiritual vocation. Today, too, many bishops and priests invest too much of their energy and time in political, socioeconomic, or ecological questions. A lack of solid theological and exegetical education, spiritual mediocrity, fear of the media, and the desire for modern society's approval also explain why some pastors have often neglected to teach the Faith; hence the necessity and urgency today of reminding them insistently about their primary duty to be messengers of the Word of God and to learn to fulfill this duty boldly, zealously, and competently. Christ Himself sends us pastors ahead of Him on a mission, as the

---

[113] Augustine, Letter 243, 8, trans. Roland Teske, S.J., in *The Works of Saint Augustine*, volume II/4 (Hyde Park, New York: New City Press, 2005), 167–168.

Gospel of Luke itself says: "After this the Lord appointed seventy others, and sent them on ahead of him, two by two, into every town and place where he himself was about to come" (Lk 10:1). Pastors, therefore, must prepare the ways of the Lord.

We can appreciate today the strength of this famous, energetic homily that Gregory the Great addressed to an assembly of bishops convoked at the Lateran, which is, so to speak, an invitation to a genuine pastoral examination of conscience. The homilist deplores the silence and inertia of many pastors in his time. But what he wrote in the sixth century is terribly relevant. His words still resound vigorously today:

> Let us listen to what the Lord says as he sends the preachers forth: "The harvest is great but the laborers are few. Pray therefore the Lord of the harvest to send laborers into his harvest." We can speak only with a heavy heart of so few laborers for such a great harvest, for although there are many to hear the good news there are only a few to preach it. Look about you and see how full the world is of priests, yet in God's harvest a laborer is rarely to be found; for although we have accepted the priestly office, we do not fulfill its demands.[114]

What would he say today with four hundred thousand priests in the world? Are we not obliged to repeat his words: "The world is full of priests, yet in God's harvest a laborer is rarely to be found!" Sometimes the pastors are unworthy of being heard, because of their sins and scandalous life; sometimes the faithful do not deserve to hear the Word of Truth. Worse yet: there are many who, as soon

---

[114] Saint Gregory the Great, *Homily on the Gospels*, in *Liturgy of the Hours*, 4:367–368.

as they take on the authority to govern, burn with the desire to tear their subjects apart, to intimidate them with their authority, to create an atmosphere of suspicion and fear, to humiliate and to harm those whom they ought to serve. And because they have no charity in their hearts, they fill their mouths with words about mercy; they pretend to be caring while completely forgetting that they are fathers.

The people are dying, and we pastors must remember that we are responsible for their spiritual death. It says to the pastors who are sent on mission: "You are the salt of the earth.... You are the light of the world" (Mt 5:13–14). Therefore, if the people are God's food, the priests ought to have been the seasoning for this food. Alas, the salt has become insipid, tasteless. Nevertheless, Saint Gregory the Great will not give up his attempts to revive the missionary zeal of pastors. He questions us relentlessly:

> Let us reflect: whom did our words convert one day? Whom did our reprimands cause to renounce their wicked actions and do penance for them? Who abandoned debauchery thanks to our instructions? Who left the path of avarice, pride, and the idolatry of natural wealth?

Conclusion

The Joy of Being a Priest

— ∞ —

In these meditations, I wanted to give the podium to the saints, to the popes—in a word, to the Church. Allow me to add in conclusion a more personal note. I would like to confide something to you. Every day, every morning and every evening, I am amazed by the grace that God gave me in calling me to be a priest. Every day, I am surprised: How could Jesus Christ bend down and regard my misery? Why did He choose as His priest, me, the little child from Ourous? Why did He come looking for me in my tiny village in Guinea? Why me, an ignorant, unworthy creature? Every day I appreciate the gratuitous, undeserved gift that He bestowed on me. This daily awareness is an ongoing source of peace and joy. Yes, every day I can celebrate the Holy Sacrifice of the Mass, every day I ascend Calvary with Christ. Every day I die with Him on the Cross. Every day I pray with Him, I intercede for the whole world by chanting the hours of the breviary. The Liturgy of the Hours is an extraordinary treasure, because it makes us stand constantly, with the whole Church, in the presence of God to praise Him and serve Him. Daily prayer and adoration before the

Most Blessed Sacrament are the heart of the priest's life and his principal activity.

Is this a weight too heavy for us poor human beings? Of course. But when Jesus loads His Cross on our shoulders, He carries it with us. I would like to recall an indelible memory from my life as a priest. In February 1992, Saint John Paul II came to Guinea for an apostolic journey, which was a popular triumph. On February 25, 1992, the saintly pope ordained three priests during a Mass celebrated in the sports stadium in the capital. In his homily, he spoke strong words that still resound in my soul:

> The cup from which Christ drank was his bloody sacrifice on Golgotha. Through this sacrifice, Christ the Servant accomplished the redemption of the world. In this way the words addressed by Christ to his disciples were completely fulfilled: the Son of man "did not come to be served, but to serve and to give his life in ransom for the multitude." A priest who celebrates the sacrifice of the Body and Blood of Christ must enter into the same spirit of service: "He will be a slave, just like the Son of man." The priesthood that you receive, dear Sons, is the sacrament of service: serve God by serving the People of God, your brothers and sisters among whom you have been called.
>
> In responding joyfully to this call, you are making a fine commitment: freely and unreservedly you offer your person to the Lord for his Church. You give up starting a family and you consecrate yourselves entirely, so as to be available fully and purely. You promise humble obedience to the bishop who is calling you to Holy Orders, and, through him, you submit to the Church and to Christ so as to take your part in the common mission with the whole

presbyterate. You make a commitment to participate faithfully in the Church's prayer, so that your ministry might be inspired and made fruitful by your intimacy with the Lord.

This ministry unites you in a particular way to Christ, the one Priest of the New Covenant, the eternal Priest. The imposition of hands consecrates you wholly and entirely through the gift of the Holy Spirit; through the anointing of your hands it is granted to you to offer the Eucharistic Sacrifice to God in Christ's name (*in persona Christi*). The whole mission of a priest is centered on the Eucharistic Sacrifice. By participating day after day in the Savior's supreme offering, a priest offers with him all of humankind to the Father, who loves it. Priests, you who have the responsibility to act in Christ's name, remain imbued with his love and keep bringing his gifts to your encounters and your various activities. Following the Lord's example, be close to the humblest, listen, relieve sufferings, and share in the joys of your brothers and sisters. In this way you will be witnesses of the Word of Life in the world.

By celebrating Christ's Sacrifice, you will come to care for the salvation of the souls that will be entrusted to you, the care of the Good Shepherd. This is why the Apostle Paul speaks to you through the words that he addressed to his disciple Timothy: "I charge you in the presence of God and of Christ Jesus ...: preach the word, be urgent in season and out of season, convince, rebuke, and exhort, be unfailing in patience and in teaching." Do not be discouraged when people "turn away from listening to the truth." Do not be discouraged. "As for you, always be steady, endure suffering, do the work of an evangelist, fulfil your ministry" [2 Tim 4:2–5].

On the evening of that day, after a meeting with young Guineans, the pope crowned the statue of the Blessed Virgin that stands in the replica of the Lourdes grotto in the gardens of the archbishop's residence. I still see him kneeling before the Mother of God, whom he loved so much. He remained silent for a long time, as though immersed in profound, intense prayer. All in attendance were struck by the intensity of that silent, solemn moment. He seemed to want to introduce and initiate us into a deep, filial devotion to Mary, the Mother of Jesus and the Mother of the priesthood. John Paul II wanted to teach us that everything comes to us through Mary, as Saint Bernard said:

> See, my brothers, with what sentiments of devotion God wanted us to honor Mary, since he placed in her the fullness of all good. If in us there is any hope, any grace, any pledge of salvation, let us acknowledge that it all pours out on us from Her who is showered with delights and graces.... Remove this sun that illumines the world, and daylight is gone. Take away Mary, the Star of the sea, from our great, vast sea, and what remains but deep obscurity, a shadow of death, and thick darkness? Therefore we must honor the Virgin Mary from the innermost recesses of our hearts, from the very depths of our being, and with our whole will; for this is the will of Him who decided that we should have everything through Her.[115]

Strengthened by this teaching, we do not hesitate to declare that an apostle, whatever he may do for the fruitfulness of his apostolate, runs the risk of building on sand

[115] Bernard, *Sermon on the Nativity of the B.V.M.*, also called *De Aquaeductu*.

unless his activity is based on a very special devotion to Our Lady.[116]

This is the teaching that Pope John Paul II wanted to leave to the laymen and the priests of Guinea and of the whole world. When he stood up again, he slowly walked over to me and put on my shoulders the stole that he was wearing. I was dumbfounded and could not understand the meaning of his gesture. It took me some time to interpret it. Indeed, through the person of the pope, it was as though Christ spoke to me again the words of my ordination. Once again, Christ, through His Church, clothed me with the stole. Jesus said to me: "Go, be the shepherd of my sheep, love them, lead them, teach them, and above all feed them with my Body and Blood." And at the same time, it was as if He said to me: "Carry the burden on your shoulders; if you abide with me it will be easy and light. Take my Cross on your shoulders. Come with me to save souls!"

Dear brother priests, this is what Jesus told you the day when you received the stole on your shoulders. This is what He says to you again every time you put it on again to celebrate Mass or a sacrament. The stole is our joy because it is the sign of our calling. On that day, John Paul II said to me by this gesture: "Do not be discouraged." He said to all of us, dear friends: "Do not be discouraged, even if people seem unwilling to listen to or to hear the Word of Truth. Do not be discouraged. Continue to walk, to carry the Cross with Christ. Do not be discouraged. In the depths of your soul keep the joy of being a humble, faithful servant of the Redeemer. Do not be discouraged!"

[116] Dom Jean-Baptiste Chautard, *L'âme de tout Apostolat* (Paris: Éditions Artège, 2010), 330–331.

For Eternity

Of course, there is no lack of sufferings and sorrows in the life of a priest. Anxiety for all the churches sometimes weighs on us (2 Cor 11:28). But nothing could overcome our profound joy. Nothing could separate us from Christ the Priest. Humanly speaking, a priest is sometimes exhausted, overwhelmed, abandoned like Jesus on Golgotha, but he is never desperate. For we know that we do not count solely on our own strength. It can be inadequate. He, Christ, will always be faithful. He will always be with us. He will always give priests to His Church. He will always remain the joy, the one joy, of His priests. On some days the Church resembles a boat that is about to be shipwrecked, but we know that Christ is present in it even though He seems to be asleep. Similarly, in our priestly heart, even though He seems to remain silent, Christ our joy always remains present and will dwell there *for eternity*.

About the Author

Cardinal Robert Sarah was born in Ourous, Guinea, in 1945 and was ordained a priest in Conakry in 1969. He then earned a licentiate in theology at the Pontifical Gregorian University in Rome and a licentiate in Scripture at the "Studium Biblicum Franciscanum" in Jerusalem.

He served as rector of the minor seminary of Kindia and as a parish priest in Bokè, Katace, Koundara, and Ourous. In 1979, he was appointed archbishop of Conakry at the age of thirty-four, making him the youngest bishop in the world.

In 2001, he was appointed Secretary of the Congregation for the Evangelization of Peoples, and in 2010, he was named President of the Pontifical Council "Cor Unum." In 2010, Pope Benedict XVI named him a Cardinal of the Church.

From 2014 to 2021, Cardinal Sarah served as Prefect of the Congregation of Divine Worship and the Discipline of the Sacraments. He has served in the Congregation for the Causes of Saints and on the Pontifical Committee for the International Eucharistic Congress. He also participated in the conclave of March 2013, which elected Pope Francis.